T0339647

Clusters, Digital Transformation and Regional Development in Germany

The information age is reshaping current socio-economic structures and processes, and this book touches upon the nature of clusters in the fourth industrial revolution (Industry 4.0; I4.0). This book focuses on the spatial perspective of digital business transformation and explores in natural context the inter-relations between cluster and I4.0. It investigates the role of knowledge, business relations and policy in making cluster relevant for I4.0 and uses the case study method and literature review to develop a conceptual framework outlining the functioning of I4.0 cluster.

This book argues that locally embedded knowledge accompanied by strong presence of industry and assisted by proper governance management facilitate the implementation of I4.0. The idiosyncrasies of I4.0 impact also the functioning of cluster as they require more inter-disciplinary integrative approach with the provision of industrial commons and development of related varieties. Natural processes of stretching of the cluster cannot be prevented but should be harnessed for upgrading the core competences of cluster. This book can enrich existing literature on economic geography and regional studies by discussing the spatial aspects of digital transformation.

It shows the cluster transformation as induced by the digital transformation and will be of interest to researchers, academics, policymakers and students, who explore the regional and local development, competitiveness or managerial aspects of I4.0.

Marta Götz is Researcher and Associate Professor at the Faculty of Business and International Relations at the Vistula University in Warsaw, Poland.

Routledge Focus on Business and Management

The fields of business and management have grown exponentially as areas of research and education. This growth presents challenges for readers trying to keep up with the latest important insights. *Routledge Focus on Business and Management* presents small books on big topics and how they intersect with the world of business research.

Individually, each title in the series provides coverage of a key academic topic, whilst collectively, the series forms a comprehensive collection across the business disciplines.

Management in the Non-Profit Sector
A Necessary Balance between Values, Responsibility and Accountability
Renato Civitillo

Fearless Leadership
Managing Fear, Leading with Courage and Strengthening Authenticity
Morten Novrup Henriksen and Thomas Lundby

Clusters, Digital Transformation and Regional Development in Germany
Marta Götz

Gender Bias in Organisations
From the Arts to Individualised Coaching
Gillian Danby and Malgorzata Ciesielska

Entrepreneurship Development in India
Debasish Biswas and Chanchal Dey

For more information about this series, please visit: www.routledge.com/ Routledge-Focus-on-Business-and-Management/book-series/FBM

Clusters, Digital Transformation and Regional Development in Germany

Marta Götz

Routledge
Taylor & Francis Group

NEW YORK AND LONDON

First published 2021
by Routledge
605 Third Avenue, New York, NY 10158

and by Routledge
2 Park Square, Milton Park, Abingdon, Oxon, OX14 4RN

Routledge is an imprint of the Taylor & Francis Group, an informa business

© 2021 Taylor & Francis

Library of Congress Cataloging-in-Publication Data
Names: Götz, Marta, author.
Title: Clusters, Digital Transformation and Regional Development in Germany / Marta Götz.
Description: New York, NY: Routledge, 2021. | Series: Routledge focus on business and management | Includes bibliographical references and index.
Identifiers: LCCN 2021001053 (print) | LCCN 2021001054 (ebook) | ISBN 9780367435158 (hardback) | ISBN 9781003005506 (ebook)
Subjects: LCSH: Industrial clusters—Germany. | Industrial location—Germany. | Electronic commerce—Germany.
Classification: LCC HC290.5.D5 G68 2021 (print) | LCC HC290.5.D5 (ebook) | DDC 338.8/7—dc23
LC record available at https://lccn.loc.gov/2021001053
LC ebook record available at https://lccn.loc.gov/2021001054

ISBN: 978-0-367-43515-8 (hbk)
ISBN: 978-1-032-03059-3 (pbk)
ISBN: 978-1-003-00550-6 (ebk)

Typeset in Times New Roman
by Apex CoVantage, LLC

Contents

Acknowledgements

This volume benefited from Bekker Programme of the Polish National Agency for Academic Exchange (NAWA)—decision no. PPN/BEK/2018/1/00034/DEC/1.

I thank the interviewees from it's OWL cluster and HAv cluster who gave their time to discuss this topic; without them, the research would not have been possible. Findings presented in this volume are researchers' interpretations of analysed phenomenon.

Part I
Setting the Stage

1 Introduction—Background of the Research and the Methodology Adopted

Opening Remarks and Context of the Study

The information age is reshaping current socio-economic structures and processes. Despite being at the centre of the policy agenda, and in business circles, Industry 4.0 (I4.0) has so far attracted proportionally less research and scholarly attention (Muscio & Ciffolilli, 2019). This volume examines the nature of clusters in the fourth industrial revolution (I4.0). It focuses on the spatial perspective of digital business transformation and explores, in natural context, the co-relations between cluster and I4.0.

Industry 4.0 stands for the digital transformation of business models and enables the fusion of virtual and real worlds (Kagermann, Wahlster & Helbig, 2013). It encompasses a set of inter-related and inter-disciplinary technologies and heralds a far-reaching integration of processes and systems, along with the emergence of the industrial internet, integrated industry or collaborative manufacturing. The Internet of Things, Internet of Services and Cyber-Physical Systems and Smart Factory are four pillars of I4.0. Clusters, on the other hand, are geographic concentrations of interconnected companies (Porter, 2000) and hybrid forms residing somewhere between hierarchies and markets (Maskell & Lorenzen, 2003), characterised by *co-opetition*. Higher competitiveness and innovative capabilities render these places attractive locations (Ketels, 2004; Malmberg & Maskell, 1999). The tension between a cluster and digital transformation, or specifically I4.0, which can lead to mass manufacturing migration, reflects the clash between the nature of these two categories, i.e. stickiness and diffusion (Buciuni & Pisano, 2015).

This study borrows from the conceptual categories of evolutionary economic geography and draws from the field of international business, especially when it refers to the global production networks (Hassink & Gong, 2017). Digitalisation, understood as the application of digital technologies and infrastructures in economies and society, has led to the emergence of a novel and distinctively different type of cluster, namely, the 'entrepreneurial ecosystem' (Autio, Nambisan, Thomas & Wright, 2018). This volume can be regarded as touching upon this issue as well, as it focuses, specifically, on the I4.0 clusters (as officially classified). It examines the cluster transformation in business digital transformation—the mutually reinforcing evolution (co-evolution) of clusters and I4.0.

Conceptual Framework and Research Design

The discussion presented in this volume is framed in *industrial commons* (IC) and *related variety* (RV) concepts and processes of *stretching* encompassing— *hubbing* and *blending*, which signify the expansion of scale and scope, respectively. It touches upon the issues of competitiveness and innovativeness, as they revolve around clusters (seen as a factor critical for competitiveness) and I4.0 (regarded as a disruptive innovation in production and business models). This text employs the case study method and presents two German I4.0 clusters, which can be seen as role models. Starting with the exploration of three major factors, namely: knowledge generation and dissemination, business relations and policy assistance—which make the cluster attractive for implementation of I4.0, this book develops a conceptual model of cluster transformation induced by the digital transformation.

The first part of the research was conducted in it's OWL cluster and is based mainly on the results of in-depth interviews held in February, 2018, in Paderborn and Lemgo, with seven cluster representatives—managers and scholars (anonymised as E1–E7). It yielded a conceptual framework, which integrates the provision of RV, IC by I4.0 cluster with *stretching* processes. It then frames the further exploration of Hamburg Aviation (HAv) cluster, which also employs a qualitative empirical research design. This study is of an exploratory nature, because research on I4.0 and clusters seems to lack a comprehensive and systematic investigation.

Germany is regarded as a leader and front-runner in adopting the fourth industrial revolution, so I have drawn two case studies from it, namely, two leading-edge clusters—it's OWL and HAv, as they could provide evidence which might be regarded as best practice. The in-depth, semi-structured interviews allow me to unearth the intricacies of the cluster transformation in digital transformation, to shed light on the nuances of mutual relations, and finally, to illuminate the specific nature of cluster in I4.0 and the relationships between these two.

Both central categories—clusters and I4.0—are critical driving forces for competitiveness. So, a better understanding of these two, and the interdependencies between them, seems crucial for regional development and broader economic growth. The emerging pattern of the reverse I4.0 impact on the cluster attributes can be established and described. It might be argued that clusters in the I4.0 age would become more inter-regional and cross-sectoral, less geographically anchored, and more diverse in terms of industrial activity.

Methodology Adopted

From the methodological perspective, this volume integrates both the richness of the context and the depth of explanation. It seeks to combine the interpretative sense-making in a natural experiment setting (Welch, Piekkari, Plakoyiannaki & Paavilainen-Mäntymäki, 2011). By framing the discussion in hybrid form of a grounded theory method (GTM—combining the Glasers' 'spontaneous grounding in empirics' with Strauss and Corbins' 'rigorous systemising'), this volume develops the conceptual model embedded in real-life data and further fills it by drawing on the real case study (Glaser & Strauss, 1967, 2011; Corbin & Strauss, 1990, 2008; Charmaz, 2009; Eisenhardt, 1989, 1991). In contrast to the rigorous and systematic, adopted here, the narrative literature review (Gancarczyk & Bohatkiewicz, 2018) allows us to identify the pluralities of a studied phenomenon.

Semi-structured, in-depth, expert interviews are the primary source of empirical data (Kiel, Voigt & Müller, 2018). The qualitative approach allows scholars to learn about complex phenomena, which are specific to the setting (Karafyllia & Zucchella, 2017; Dominguez & Mayrhofer, 2017; Vanninen, Kuivalainen & Ciravegna, 2017; Eisenhardt, 1989, 1991; Zaefarian, Eng & Tasavori, 2016; Eisenhardt & Graebner, 2007; Yin, 2009). The case study with phenomenon-driven selection offers valuable contextual data, insight and knowledge, which could not have been gained otherwise (Flyvbjerg, 2006; Martineau & Pastoriza, 2016; Kasabov, 2015; Fletcher, Zhao, Plakoyiannaki & Buck, 2018; Fletcher & Plakoyiannaki, 2011; Patton, 2015; Schurink & Auriacombe, 2010).

Interviews in the HAv cluster, in Spring 2019, were held with representatives from the HAv office, Hamburg City (Ministry of Economy), research institutions, scholars from Helmut Schmidt and Christian Albrecht Universities in Kiel, as well as managers or CEOs of various companies. These are mainly small and medium-sized, often start-ups, active in consulting, training, productions and design. This study certainly benefited from consultations with IfW experts and the insight acquired during the 55th Hamburg Aviation Forum. The interviewers were anonymised and classified as cluster representatives (CRs), or cluster HAv experts (CEs), cluster companies (CCs), cluster officials (COs), cluster scholars (CSs), respectively. The sample of companies which took part in this study is pretty heterogeneous and comprises start-ups, small- and medium-sized enterprises (SMEs), subsidiaries of large multinational companies, as well as representing different tiers of the supply chain.

This study used manual coding, without the assistance of any software, to preserve the narrative integrity of the transcripts and assure the interpretation of text sections within the context of the rest of the conversation (8; Cao, Navare & Jin, 2018; McHenry & Welch, 2018). Constantly rotating between the necessary analysis and collection of data makes the whole process recursive rather than linear (Spieth & Meissner Née Schuchert, 2018) and enabled identification of first-order codes, establishing second-order constructs and finally, the aggregate dimensions (Tzeng, 2018; Cao, Navare & Jin, 2018; Gioia, Corley & Hamilton, 2013).

Summing up, this study adopts the qualitative abductive 'in vivo' approach, which builds upon the pre-existing categories and aims at seeing 'the general in particular' (McHenry & Welch, 2018). It extends from classic inductive theory building towards the contextualised explanation (Welch, Piekkari, Plakoyiannaki & Paavilainen-Mäntymäki, 2011). It strives to address the principles of relational research design, which generate abstract and transferable findings, whereas acknowledging contingent conditions of a given setting (Bathelt & Glückler, 2018). As a conceptual tool, the relational approach helps to overcome the separation between different disciplinary perspectives and facilitates cross-disciplinary engagement.

Contribution to Current Research

This volume explores in a natural context ('in vivo'—a case study), the (changing?) nature of clusters in the I4.0 era and the local/geographic dimension of I4.0. It indirectly addresses the unresolved, classic dilemma of specialisation versus diversification and fits into the debate on striking a balance between the local and global aspects of clusters (i.e. how to reconcile local embeddedness with global openness). It enriches our knowledge on cluster attractiveness in the age of digital transformation and advances our understanding of a cluster's characteristics, likely to determine the adoption of I4.0.

This book can offer some guidelines for policymakers, cluster managers and all those involved in shaping the regional aspects of digital transformation and responsible for regional technology and innovation policies. It tackles the issue of cluster dynamics, though not explicitly, as it incorporates the ongoing fourth industrial revolution and accounts for the I4.0 impact on cluster conceptualisation. Recent research on the cluster demonstrated that a static approach to clusters suffers many shortcomings, and a dynamic evolutionary perspective is necessary (Belussi & Hervas-Oliver, 2016). The discussed problems address the issues raised as emergent lines in current cluster research, such as internationalisation, sustainability or relatedness and variety (Lazzeretti, Capone, Caloffi & Sedita, 2019).

The value-added of the volume consists of integrating the space with technology; of combining clusters and I4.0 so far, although often covered in scholarly papers, and much discussed by policymakers as sources of competitiveness and innovativeness, treated separately (Spaini et al., 2019). Whereas, clusters are with us for some decades; explored and studied at various levels, and from different perspectives, using multiple methods; the fourth industrial revolution is something of a new topic (Schwab, 2017, Hannover Messe 2011, or 2016 Davos World Economic Forum; Visvizi & Lytras, 2019). Nevertheless, the research on this topic is mushrooming and growing, exponentially. That being said, the technological and engineering aspects seem to dominate the ongoing discussion. The business or managerial aspects have taken off only recently, whereas other dimensions, such as spatial or geographical aspects of I4.0, seem to remain an uncharted area. This volume touches upon this somewhat neglected topic so far—the cluster-I4.0 interplay.

2 Industry 4.0 and the Contribution of Clusters for the Advancing I4.0

The Fourth Industrial Revolution (I4.0)

Industry 4.0, or the fourth industrial revolution (I4.0), as it is otherwise known, is seen by some as a business model's transformation, by others as a state-sponsored vision of modern manufacturing, as a disruption in production processes or a fusion of cyber and real worlds (Kagermann, Wahlster & Helbig, 2013; Smit, Kreutzer, Moeller & Carlberg, 2016). This term is narrower than the general megatrend of digitalisation as it refers to the broadly understood manufacturing processes. I4.0 often applied synonymously—Smart Manufacturing, Smart Production or the Internet of Things—has been identified as substantial pillars of the digital and automated manufacturing environment (Kamble, Gunasekaran & Gawankar, 2018). I4.0 encompasses a variety of technologies, which allow for the development of the value chains, ensuing reduced manufacturing lead times, better product quality and organisational performance. I4.0's related developments have given rise to much interest in recent literature. However, few systematic reviews seek to capture the dynamic nature of this topic (Maresova et al., 2018; Pereira, Santos & Cleto, 2018; Benitez, Ferreira Lima, Lerman & Frank, 2019). I4.0 seen as a business-to-business (B2B) interface of digital transformation stands for disruptive innovation in production systems or a set of ground-breaking technologies transforming the markets. It is also perceived in terms of modern industrial policy. I4.0 refers to a radical change in production technology (Schuh, Potente, Wesch-Potente, Weber & Prote, 2014; Strange & Zucchella, 2017; Philbeck & Davis, 2019). Although the effects of this change will be characterised as revolutionary, when considered in retrospect, their impact on existing manufacturing operations will be more gradual (Szalavetz, 2019). The path to the I4.0 model will, therefore, be an evolutionary one.

The cyber-physical systems (CPS), or cyber-physical production systems (CPPS), also called intelligent technical systems (ITSs), form the basis of I4.0 (Gouarderes, 2016; Roblek, Meško & Krapež, 2016; Brettel, Friederichsen, Keller & Rosenberg, 2014; Hermann, Pentek & Otto, 2015). I4.0

stands for embedded systems, which are crucial for advanced specialised production for factory outfitters and technology leaders. Thanks to ITS, value chains can be re-organised, monitored and controlled (Hüther, 2016; Liao, Deschamps, de Freitas, Loures & Ramos, 2017; Manyika et al., 2016; Rüßmann et al., 2015). Investments in I4.0 can translate into more sustainability, thanks to facilitating eco-efficiency and contributing to the circular economy (De Marchi & Di Maria, 2019). ITSs are complex products that build upon the interaction between information technology and engineering, with software components integrated into machinery and equipment. ITS needs to be adaptive, robust, predictive and user-friendly, and then it will allow various benefits to unfold. Resources are used more efficiently, and production can be individualised and customised. Reliability, safety and availability of products are enhanced, the development installation and management improved and products get new functionalities (Industrie 4.0, Studie BITKOM; Industrie 4.0, smart manufacturing for the future, 2014; International: Industry 4.0 will arrive unevenly, 2016).

MAKERS experts (www.makers-rise.org/about/) advocate a modified approach to I4.0 as a new way of organising production between firms, as well as new business models, but also new ways of communicating with consumers and users, along with new ways of using and consuming products. Economy 4.0 means that various stakeholders—workers, employers, communities, firms and consumers engage in consumption and production. EU-wide I4.0 should be seen as a cross-cutting agenda. Reischauer (2018) argues for viewing I4.0 as a policy-driven discourse, which aims at institutionalising innovation systems, as presented by a triple helix, i.e. made up of business, academia and politics.

There is no official universal classification of I4.0 activities and related technologies in the literature (Santos, Mehrsai, Barros, Araújo & Ares, 2017; Ciffolilli & Muscio, 2018). Nevertheless, as a proxy of I4.0, the key enabling technologies (KETs) can be adopted, including Additive Manufacturing, Augmented Reality Simulation Horizontal/Vertical Integration, Cloud or Big Data and Analytics. Based on data on European regions' participation in the 7th Framework Programme, Ciffolilli and Muscio (2018) reveal that Germany is a solitary leader in I4.0 research and technology development, both in terms of project co-ordination and involvement, enjoying broader participation of national firms in collaborative endeavours. Hence, it seems reasonable to focus the exploration on the German case, and in particular, on the German I4.0 clusters.

Clusters Potential Role in I4.0

Clusters are defined as geographic concentrations of interconnected companies, specialised suppliers, service providers and associated institutions, active in a particular field that are present in a nation or a region (Porter, 2000). They are seen as hybrid forms of long-term contracting, reciprocal trading, residing somewhere between hierarchies and markets (Maskell & Lorenzen, 2003). Clusters are attractive business locations commonly associated with multiple advantages. Simultaneous co-opetition among firms and their co-operation with universities, scientific bodies and regional authorities, create synergies, while fostering innovativeness and competitiveness (Keeble & Wilkinson, 2000; Kogut & Zander, 1992; Cantwell, 1989; Dahl, Pedersen & Dalum, 2003; Barry, Goerg & Strobl, 2003; Basile, Benfratello & Castellani, 2003; Belderbos & Carree, 2002; Cieślik, 2004; Coughlin & Segev, 1997; Guimaraes, Figueiredo & Woodward, 2000; Head, Ries & Swenson, 1999).

The traditional thinking sees clusters as vertical, sectorally specialised 'silos' (James & Halkier, 2016), but nowadays, clusters can span sectoral boundaries and are based around common markets or shared technologies (Delgado, Porter & Stern, 2016; Puig, 2019). James and Halkier (2016, p. 832) stress the necessity 'to identify novel directions of industrial knowledge flows, by-passing these specialised "silos", to horizontal and combinatorial "platforms"'. In this spirit, Suwala and Micek (2018) developed a novel perspective on regional transformation. They proposed symbiotic co-existence of strategies for cluster-based 'smart-specialisation' and platform-based 'diversification', which can be called 'smart diversification'. This new strategy might be referred to as 'beyond clusters', but it is definitively not a 'post-cluster' approach.

Clusters tend to be harnessed as vehicles for transformation and competitiveness upgrading as it seems the need for evolution of the cluster might be even more urgent under I4.0 pressure. We may indeed witness more diversified and more dispersed clusters. The studied concepts of '*blending*' and '*hubbing*' illuminate the need to see the evolution of clusters as being linked to the processes of scale and scope (Njøs, Orre & Fløysand, 2017). The diversified specialisation might be the outcome of cluster policy aiming at 'specialisation in diversification' (Benner, 2017). In the light of I4.0-induced transformation, the cluster might be deprived of its geographic attributes. What might matter, would be the network's embeddedness, and not necessarily, the geographic collocation and spatial proximity. It might be hypothesised that clusters, due to I4.0 idiosyncrasies (inter-disciplinary and integrative properties), would become less spatially concentrated and less specialised.

At first sight, the concepts of cluster and advanced smart manufacturing, as envisaged by I4.0, are incompatible. I4.0 heralds 'producing anything anywhere', whereas the cluster ties the activity to one particular location. The previous study revealed, however, different channels of influence and outlined the ways, in which clusters can facilitate the advancement of I4.0 (Götz & Jankowska, 2017). Idiosyncrasies of knowledge creation and subsequent dissemination, which are fundamental for I4.0, can be reconciled with the unique features of innovation processes taking place in clusters. New business models triggered by the fourth industrial revolution, epitomised by the concepts of the connected company with vanishing boundaries, or the digital business ecosystems, might be identified in mechanisms associated with clusters. I4.0 proclaims a specific organisational shift towards highly adaptive networks of inter-related entities and stipulates the re-organisation of markets towards the platform structures. In this context, clusters seem to be pre-destined to serve as centres and nodes in such configurations. Finally, clusters can be applied as a promising policy tool, organising the implementation of the fourth industrial revolution and securing a more co-ordinated and smoother digital transformation of business. It appears that a digital revolution, which is influencing global value chains (GVCs), networks and expectations towards manufacturing firms, is turning our attention to clusters as the appropriate environments. For IT-assisted and globally spread operations of I4.0, co-location still remains essential, as multiple advantages, provided by clusters, facilitate the development and implementation of I4.0. Clusters can certainly be harnessed as laboratories for I4.0 experiments. They offer a favourable environment, stimulating knowledge creation and its further diffusion, and can function as a policy tool enabling the implementation of advanced projects, while also being seen as nodes in the architecture of platforms or networks. Thus, it might be argued that cluster attributes address the imminent challenges of I4.0 and that the properties of clusters are aligned with I4.0-specific requirements.

Part II

On the Role of Knowledge, Business Relations and Policy in Making Cluster Relevant for Industry 4.0

3 Intelligent Technical Systems

OstWestfalen-Lippe—It's OWL Cluster

It's OWL Facts and Figures

The German region, OstWestfalen-Lippe (OWL), in the state of North Rhine-Westphalia, hosting it's OWL leading-edge cluster, can be regarded as the best practice homeland for the development of I4.0. It implements the idea of smart specialisation, where natural bottom-up advantages are met with top-down support. OWL is 'at the top of North Rhine-Westphalia', not only in geographical terms, but also economically. The region is one of the most active commercial areas in Germany. It is marked by outstanding value added and employment in the mechanical engineering, electrical and electronics industries, as well as the automotive supply sector. It can boast a broad industrial mix, with a focus on the manufacturing sector, medium-sized, family-run firms and a dynamic research community based on the field of ITSs, which offers companies direct access to cutting-edge research.

It's OWL is one of the 15 recent winners of the Leading-Edge Cluster Competition, initiated by the Federal Ministry of Education and Research (BMBF), which becomes a flagship high-tech strategy of federal government (Rothgang et al., 2017; Deutschlands Spitzencluster, 2014). It was intended to be a regional pooling of economy and science along the value chain.

So far altogether, 47 projects and 171 transfer projects have been conducted. Companies have created around 7,500 new jobs since 2012, apart from 34 business start-ups, representing an area of flexible production which has been set up (Who makes SMEs ready for the digital future?, 2019).

The core competences of it's OWL are mechanical engineering, electrical/electronics and automotive supply industries. The business population consists of strong brands, hidden champions (HCs), many SMEs and independent family owned companies. Research builds on the symbiosis of IT and engineering sciences. There are 22 main industry partners (investment in innovation projects), 86 associated companies (co-operation in transfer projects), 24 engineering and consulting companies (multipliers), 17 universities and research institutes, 30 economy-oriented organisations (courtesy of the representative of it's OWL Cluster management GmbH, 2018). To remain competitive, the cluster is seeking international co-operation, for instance, by forging strategic partnerships with relevant foreign cluster partners, such as DIMECC (www.dimecc.com) (Finland). The region positions itself as the enabler for I4.0 and Digitalisation. The cutting-edge cluster—it's OWL—pools technologies, which are essential for innovative leaps, in the form of technology platform generated during the cross-sectional projects. This platform enables the subsequent technology transfer, and thereby facilitates the access to I4.0, which is critical for medium-sized manufacturing firms. This unique technology is supposed to guarantee growth and employment in core industries, and secure in the long run, manufacturing production in Germany.

Knowledge Generation and Technology Transfer

The fourth industrial revolution implies that expectations towards CPS, the backbone of I4.0, are formidable, causing enormous challenges to the R&D community. Nevertheless, the interactive character of learning processes and peculiarities of knowledge generation, imply that geographical space emerges as a necessary dimension. Knowledge creation and dissemination require mutual trust, understanding, some compatibility of beliefs, close daily co-operation, shared norms or face-to-face interactions facilitated by various forms of proximity.

The importance of co-location derives from the inter-related nature of 'research-development-innovation' and production in some industries (www.makers-rise.org/about/). There is a substantial overlap in geographic concentration between GVCs and global innovation networks, and the GVC hubs are often hubs of global innovation networks. The presence of local Knowledge-Intensive Business Service (KIBS) firms proves critical for the manufacturing fabric (Vendrell-Herrero & Wilson, 2017). It can produce a virtuous circle of regional growth (Lafuente, Vaillant & Vendrell-Herrero, 2017). The business strategy, which rests on complementing the product offerings with services, is labelled as servitisation or product-service innovation (Bustinza, Vendrell-Herrero, Santini, Bellandi, & De Propris, 2017). It heralds a shift to a hybrid model, where manufacturing and services are increasingly intertwined. Inserting services to the existing business models becomes a condition '*sine qua non*', particularly for SMEs. The processes of territorial co-location and knowledge transfer between manufacturing SMEs and KIBS in Europe are confirmed in available studies (Lafuente, Vaillant & Vendrell-Herrero, 2017).

The agglomeration of both service-related knowledge and specialised manufacturing competences arise as an essential factor. As KIBS often face unique problems with some of their clients, they demand direct contacts with them, to be able to provide optimal solutions. A high share of these interactions, especially in the early stages of co-operation, reveals a tacit nature, justifying the physical proximity (Muller & Zenker, 2001). KIBS firms are supposed to enrich the existing manufacturing businesses, as well as the new ones, with advanced services (Corrocher & Cusmano, 2014; Lafuente, Vaillant & Serarols, 2010). A KIBS segment can safeguard territorial resilience, manufacturing renaissance, firms' competitiveness and regional development. Close co-operation between manufacturing and KIBS may be responsible for generating *RV*, i.e. the benefits of co-existence of diversified, yet complementary, industries (Frenken, Van Oort & Verburg, 2007).

It's OWL cluster focuses on the structure, composition and functioning of the underpinning of I4.0, i.e. the technology systems and on what makes them intelligent. ITSs consist of four units: the underlying system and the three kinds of technologies: sensor, actuator and the information processing one. The latter plays a fundamental role by binding through the communication system, the sensors and the actuators. Whereas sensors acquire, from the external environment, the critical information, actuators execute a physical action based on the core underpinning system (www.its-owl.com/fileadmin/PDF/Informationsmaterialien/2015-On_the_road_to_Industry_4.0_-_Solutions_from_the_Leading-Edge_Cluster_it_s_OWL.pdf). Such underlying systems are usually the mechanical structures—machinery or equipment. When all four units are found together, this is called a sub-system. Multiple sub-systems linked in a group (such as in a vehicle or machine tool) are called a 'system'. When systems communicate with each other and work together, regardless of physical separation, this is a networked system.

Thanks to the implementation of 47 research projects to the tune of EUR 100 million, it's OWL offers concrete products, technologies and practical solutions for using ITSs in broader industry (Who makes . . . , 2018). The core regional research focuses on cross-sectoral subjects, such as plug-and-produce, intelligent networking or energy efficiency, which are built upon the local expertise in developing sub-systems, systems and networked systems.

The goal is to leverage the knowledge obtained in innovation projects with leading firms and make it transferable to other smaller companies. This proliferation, which features high on the cluster management agenda, implies selecting (literally, 'taking out of brackets the common element'/'factor out') some current technologies identified as crucial for the development of I4.0 and making them available through the technology platforms.

The strength of the region derives, undoubtedly, from its scientific and research potential. Six universities are engaged in the Leading-Edge Cluster, it's OWL. These are Bielefeld University, Paderborn University, University of Applied Sciences Ostwestfalen-Lippe, Bielefeld University of Applied Sciences, Hamm-Lippstadt University of Applied Sciences and the private university of Applied Economic Sciences, Fachhochschule der Wirtschaft (FHDW). They are recognised for their inter-disciplinary character. First-class pure research is conducted by the Cluster of Excellence Center in Cognitive Interactive Technology (CITEC) at Bielefeld University and three collaborative research centres. Essential roles are also played by the Heinz Nixdorf Institute (Paderborn University), the CoR-Lab Research Centre for Cognition and Robotics (Bielefeld University), the Institute of Industrial IT (University of Applied Sciences Ostwestfalen-Lippe) and the Institute of System Dynamics and Mechatronics (Bielefeld University of Applied Sciences). Additionally, several research institutes, such as the Fraunhofer IEM (Paderborn) and the Fraunhofer IOSB Industrial Automation application centre (Lemgo), collaborate with business aiming to find the new applications for obtained research results. Overall, around 1,000 scientists are representing 18 research institutes and three Fraunhofer Institutes involved in ITSs research in OWL including groups such as Audi, Boeing, Fujitsu, Honda and Siemens, who have chosen to work with research institutes in the region (www.its-owl.de/de/ueber-uns/region/wissenschaft-forschung/).

It's OWL sees its role in and acts primarily as a technology platform. It serves as the basis for dissemination of knowledge and the transfer of technologies and methods developed in innovative projects and assures that they are all accessible to cluster SMEs. Various types of projects can be distinguished. Cross-sectional projects involve self-optimisation, human-machine interactions, plug-and-play; innovative projects focus on sub-systems, systems and network systems, whereas sustainability initiatives (to make companies more competitive) are based on work 4.0; forecasting, market focus or counterfeit prevention.

Representatives of it's OWL (from Lemgo—Smart Factory or Garage33), undisputedly confirm the role of spatial proximity. Daily contacts, frequent interactions and other benefits provided by co-location, imply that 'something is in the air' and there is a 'feeling of belonging'.

The technology transfer seems to be the backbone of cluster existence, given the intense research in the area and the large population of SMEs, which is one of the most strategic assets of the cluster. The starting point for refinement of the modes of technology transfer was some disappointment with existing methods. It's OWL representatives name, among other factors, the fact that most research results do not find their way to the market. Innovation needs to be measured by an increase in market share and margins, rather than publications. Many researchers are not closely inter-linked with the industry. The industry does not know enough about existing strengths in research. Joint projects to implement excellent research results are not widely spread. The smaller the companies get, the more significant becomes the gap to science/research. Best practice models are not visible enough, so most people need to 'fly their own learning curve'. Despite these clear obstacles, recognition of the benefits of co-operation, especially amongst competitors, proves feasible in the case of it's OWL. Companies, although often rivals, acknowledge the need for collaboration and sharing 'know-how', as a way to stay competitive internationally and when compared to the rivals outside the cluster.

In general, four pillars of research-related activities can be distinguished. The first one encompasses generating innovation through cutting-edge research and usually implies bilateral, high calibre, advanced, breakthrough projects between larger firms and academia. Technology transfer, or in general, the proliferation of the results of projects mentioned above, is regarded as the central element of cluster. Likewise, the development of entrepreneurship in digital industries includes technology scouting, infrastructure sharing or creating digital leadership programmes. The final crucial aspect and task of it's OWL constitutes the provision of solutions for the modern digitally transformed labour market.

The transfer usually results from actions undertaken by both sides—providers and beneficiaries, which means there is demand from the companies' side and an offer provided by the researcher, simultaneously. Often, the exchange is facilitated by some third party who carries the information and brokers the transfer later on. Many barriers can hamper the transfer. These are present on both sides, among researchers, as well as in the firms, themselves. A lack of opportunities for making contact are usually quoted, as well as: missing or insufficient information media; bad experiences from previous projects discouraging further collaboration; some prejudice against potential partners; problems with confidentiality and copyright; or a lack of capability, willingness and resources; conflicting goals; and diverging expectation concerning the schedule or unclear priorities of technology transfer. Nevertheless, it is often challenging to obtain the necessary approvals, adhere to copyrights, observe intellectual property rights and so define the terms and conditions, in order that meaningful transfer of knowledge, originating in innovative research projects, can happen. The objective of technology transfer is to provide mainly SMEs with the access to ITS development, contained in the technology platform, so that they can move from mechanical, through mechatronic, to the ITS.

Crucial areas of co-operation are self-optimisation (machine learning and maintenance), human-machine interaction (augmented reality and robotics), intelligent networking (Plug & Play), energy efficiency (energy management) and system engineering (SE) (cross-disciplinary and interface standardisation, based on material provided by courtesy of the representative of it's OWL. Cluster management GmbH, 2018, www.its-owl.com/fileadmin/PDF/Informationsmaterialien/2017-Technology_Transfer_web.pdf). Available statistics revealed that most popular are the projects in the area of mechanical engineering and construction, mechatronics and electrical technology, followed by chemistry, medical and automotive technology (Figure 3.1). Systems engineering and human-machine interactions proved to be the most important topics of these projects (Figure 3.2).

Technology transfer happens in stages. It usually starts with an overview and actions, such as information days or trade shows, and proceeds through intensifying understanding, along with specifying demands for implementing concrete solutions.

In the eyes of it's OWL members, the key for the success of these projects is the implementation of a stepwise approach, which implies going from sensitisation events to tailored transfer projects. Also critical is a close involvement of transfer multipliers, which is based on forceful contacting and integration of a wide range of SMEs. An important role is played by the setting up of technology transfer-labs, which allow for the demonstration of new technologies. Finally, successful transfer project implementations are inherently related to creating an ethos of co-operation.

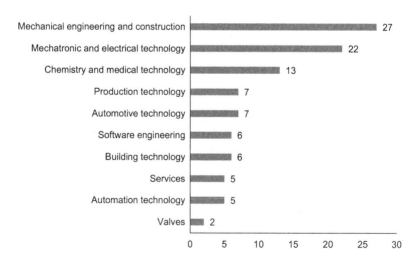

Figure 3.1 Projects conducted in it's OWL—sectors (2018)

Source: Own elaboration based on data—courtesy of the representative of it's OWL Clustermanagement GmbH, 2018

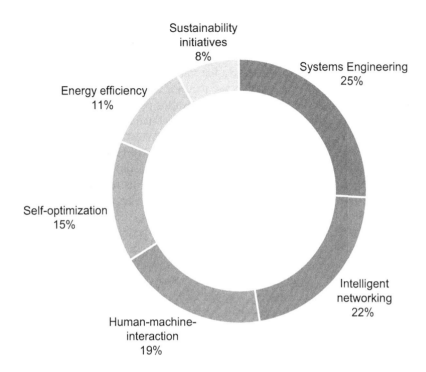

Figure 3.2 Projects conducted in it's OWL—areas (2018)

Source: Own elaboration based on data—courtesy of the representative of it's OWL Clustermanagement GmbH, 2018

Table 3.1 The four-stage technology transfer model

Transfer projects for concrete problems	Use, integration	**Vertical transfer**
Targeted workshops with selected content	Trial and testing	
Knowledge sharing groups and further training	**Deeper understanding**	**Horizontal transfer**
Transfer events, 'solutions' event programme and trade fairs	**Interest and preliminary information**	

Source: Based on material provided by courtesy of the representative of it's OWL Clustermanagement GmbH, 2018, www.its-owl.com/fileadmin/PDF/Informationsmaterialien/2017-Technology_Transfer_web.pdf

The transfer philosophy helps, not only to break down the barriers, but also to create a culture of co-operation. To assure the successful sharing of technology, it seems critical to safeguard the 'win-win' situation, so that both—the transfer providers and recipients—can benefit from such exchange. As it looks, it is precisely the transfer of technologies and dissemination of knowledge, which is the focus of it's OWL activities, rather than fostering purely research-oriented innovation projects.

It must be stressed that the cluster's role in facilitating knowledge development draws on two dimensions. The knowledge stock encompassing the rich scientific landscape, the set of research units, universities, laboratories and research institutions, such as the Fraunhofer Institute's Mechatronic and System Design, which is diversified but represents related areas, and is accompanied by the mechanisms enabling the generation and smooth dissemination of this knowledge (e.g. the technology transfer centres, or conducted projects, in the case of it's OWL: cross-sectional projects, innovative projects and sustainability initiatives). The importance of both the knowledge base and the mechanisms enabling its dissemination (access to it for a possible large pool of local actors) suggests the role played by these knowledge-related assets. They can be seen as a specific public good, which, in fact, might be understood in terms of ICs. ICs might be regarded as a particular category of cluster commons (Sölvell, 2015).

Dual Strategy—A Business Ecosystem

The core of the cluster constitutes the critical mass of companies. Business—the concentration of firms representing one or more related industries, buyers and customers, service providers and the support entities is, hence, a 'sine qua non' condition of any cluster existence. Given the transformation triggered by the I4.0, the emergence of new business models is expected. The concept of a fractal company—an open hierarchical system consisting of independent self-similar, self-organised, self-optimising goal-oriented units—may resemble the *co-opetiton* typical for clusters. The idea of a 'connected enterprise' emblematic of a new I4.0 business model can also be diagnosed in the 'modus operandi' of clusters. The cluster epitomises the broader understanding of I4.0 that must not be limited only to the digitalisation of production processes. It encompasses the whole ecosystem consisting of humans, machines, rules and organisations. The entrepreneurial digital ecosystem seems to be a pre-requisite for efficient and effective transformation towards I4.0, and clusters could offer such an environment.

As the argument of the exploitation of economies of scale seems to expire, if firms are to remain competitive, they need to deliver customisation, while at the same time, secure high levels of scalability and efficiency. They have to morph towards innovation-intensive and difficult-to-imitate business models, based on services and the digital upgrading of products. Servitisation of manufacturing (Dimache & Roche, 2013) may suggest contamination of service practices and strategies to manufacturing. It leads to new business models in production, with features such as the pervasive penetration of digital technology; increasing involvement of customers in manufacturing processes; and new relationships between manufacturing and services. The competitiveness of the manufacturing sector increasingly relies on its capability of inserting into the operation, certain value-adding services and it, therefore, depends on the possibility of providing integrated 'service-good' packages (Cusumano, Kahl & Suarez, 2015).

Regional economic performance does not just come from the regional economic specialisation or the agglomeration of firms, in purely quantitative terms. It, instead, derives from the inter-connections and complementarities. Processes of territorial servitisation can improve local competitiveness and employment through the virtuous cycle, when the local manufacturing base creates supplementary KIBS businesses, which further facilitate the emergence of new manufacturers (Lafuente, Vaillant & Vendrell-Herrero, 2017). Territorial servitisation might be seen as responsible for 'RV', as it stipulates the potential of diversification.

As diagnosed in the high-tech strategy of the German government and inferred from various reports, this transition towards I4.0 can be successful, only when a dual strategy is applied, i.e. a close interaction between factory outfitters and manufacturing companies is present (Gausemeier & Klocke, 2016). Whereas factory outfitters must position themselves as lead suppliers, to be able to adapt to production requirements, manufacturers must create markets that allow ITSs to be built and run in production.

The structure of it's OWL, dominated by both the electrical industry and mechanical and plant engineering, embodies this dual strategy. Many of the CCs, such as those globally renowned for electronic connector technology, are factory outfitters, who set standards in the field of industrial automation. These developments also benefit the machinery and equipment manufacturers, who can improve their potential for innovation, due to the use of these ITSs. Supplemented by a robust research community, it's OWL pools both the expertise (supply) and market needs (demand). It belongs to the most active production clusters in Europe, marked by a high concentration of employment and innovation capacity, as well as export quota (www. ostwestfalen-lippe.de/images/Zahlen_Daten_Fakten_OWL_2017.pdf). The region hosts 400 companies representing the mechanical, engineering, electrical and electronics industries, as well as the automotive supply industry, which employs around 80,000 individuals, and annually generates revenue to the tune of EUR 17 billion.

The cluster consists of many family-run and medium-sized firms. These include global market leaders and strong brands, such as Claas, Gildemeister, Hella, Miele and Wincor Nixdorf, but also many HCs. Beckhoff, Harting, KEB, Lenze, Phoenix Contact, Wago and Weidmüller set global standards in industrial electronics and hold 75% of the global market share for connector technology. They are unknown to the broader public but are global leaders in the niche markets. The study by Rammer and Spielkamp (2019) revealed that the HCs' competitive strategy rests on technology leadership and customisation. Although they do not invest more in innovation, they achieve higher innovation success thanks to appropriate human capital and HR management practices that mobilise the creative potential of their employees.

The OWL region is also marked by a broad mix of manufacturing industries, with a focus on the furniture, food, plastics and metal sectors, where 1,696 companies are employing 190,000 individuals, and generating revenue of EUR 38 billion (based on it's OWL materials, incl. *Who makes SMEs ready for the digital future?*, Cluster management, 2019, www.its-owl.com/fileadmin/PDF/Informationsmaterialien/2019_Infobroschuere_EN_inkl_Projekte_WEB.pdf).

These firms work together in various industry initiatives, and cluster programmes are designed and structured in a way to safeguard the highest added value and employment in the region.

The initiative Garage 33 (name due to the nearby highway number 33 and postcode of Paderborn), which started in May 2017, provides a comprehensive start-up ecosystem for local firms. Garage 33 is tasked primarily with the organisation of workshops, series of competitions or roundtables. It actively seeks and invites business angels—private companies who can invest so-called 'smart money', time and knowledge in promising initiatives. Garage 33 helps start-ups from 'A to Z', with business coaching. The concept of 'lean start-up' enables young, promising, although risky endeavours, the necessary process of testing (trial and error phase), before marketing and commercialisation. Garage 33 accompanies students, graduates or young scholars, who wish to start their own business. It organises the start-up weekends, calls for ideas, conducts live hacking, arena meetings, community parties and meet-ups. It provides scholarships and financing, networking and mentoring, by arranging so-called disruptive workshops, whose aim is to shake up the current business models and provide a breakthrough or a game-changer for a given business. All activities are always carried out according to the principle 'take and give'. Some support and learning are also possible for Garage 33 management, itself, thanks to contacts with more mature peers' initiatives, which may serve as a benchmark of best practices.

Summing up, this section seems to confirm the cluster role in assuring better efficiency of doing business, in particular, I4.0 business. Concertation of suppliers and customers, the existence of trading relations, demand-supply links, all relate to the core assumption of the dual strategy. It assumes the co-existence of factory outfitters and manufacturers; of excellent supply providers (engineering) and market creators (manufacturers), which are seen as crucial for successful digital business transformation. Whereas the supply side can benefit from scale economies—in clusters, in particular, the external scale economies and associated positive externalities can thrive; the demand side can take advantage of network effects, assuming that the more consumers are involved, the better. It's OWL gathers the representatives of various sectors and market segments. Firms come from mechanical engineering, the electrical and electronics industry, the automotive supply industry and manufacturing, and are pre-dominantly, small and medium, family-run companies, often HCs. The B2B environment seems to be, indeed, one of the critical elements of cluster attractiveness for I4.0. The idiosyncrasy of I4.0 and the cross-sectoral, horizontal attributes of it, determines that instead of specialisation, we should rather speak of RV; of the co-existence of diversified, yet complementary industries and the transformation towards smart diversification (Suwala & Micek, 2018).

Institutions and Policy—Governance of Relationships

As previous studies and German initiatives showed, clusters can be harnessed as a suitable and promising policy tool (Dohse, 2007; Dohse, Fornahl & Vehrke, 2018). Thanks to the formal and institutional framework—management, structure and governance—they may reduce the uncertainty problem, inherently related to I4.0. This uncertainty suggests the need for some risk-sharing, networking, establishing platforms of co-operation or alliances, and turn the attention to clusters, where these positive effects can be reinforced by spatial proximity.

In light of the fourth industrial revolution, policy support seems critical, as it may rebuild the competitiveness of developed economies (Fetzer, Schweitzer, & Peitz, 2017). Technological change can restore the competitiveness in mature, advanced economies, and this is where policy should be focused (OECD, 2017a, 2017b). It is of particular importance for SMEs, suffering often from the climate of mistrust, as they struggle to recognise themselves, in models that look entirely different from what they used to know. Small business in I4.0 time needs guidelines, precise definitions and more professional assistance. It seems to make sense to define the new concepts clearly, to set the right framework and offer adequate support. The need for establishing interoperability standards, also features high on the agenda. The Leading-Edge Cluster programme is a central component of the German High-Tech Strategy. Through the competition, the Federal Ministry of Education and Research (BMBF) supports the top-performing commercial and scientific clusters (Rothgang et al., 2017). It's OWL is one of the 15 winners of this prestigious contest—the strategic initiative I4.0—which has been launched, initially, to support and shape the transition to modern industry. It's OWL with 200 members is considered to be the best practice of I4.0 projects (Who makes SMEs . . . , 2019). The project, in general, and other accompanying related activities carried out are intended to safeguard and create new jobs, to establish new research institutes and businesses, to bring new scientists into the region and to set up new study programmes.

Additionally, the European Cluster Excellence Initiative (ECEI) has awarded to it's OWL, a Gold Label for its cluster management. This quality label recognised all over Europe, serves as an independent and voluntary benchmark, confirming the highest excellence of cluster management. The victory in the Federal Competition Leading Edge and distinction granted by the ECEI, furthermore, bolster the quality of services, organisation and co-ordination provided by the cluster team.

All these rewards are the sign of recognition of the excellence of cluster management. As stressed by it's OWL officials, the robust governance model applied cannot be under-estimated, as it, indeed, enables the achievement of ambitious goals. The balanced stakeholders' structure and cluster board, who enjoy a strong mandate to represent the firms, to speak on their behalf, to enter negotiations with their legitimacy and make binding agreements, as well as the right division of tasks among the management, marketing and R&D teams, contribute to the success.

The management company—it's OWL Cluster management GmbH—is responsible for project implementation, development of strategy, as well as marketing activities and networking practices among its partners. The task of the executive board, i.e. the cluster board, is to determine the strategic direction of it's OWL evolution. A scientific advisory board provides recommendations and guidance regarding future technology platforms. Experts stemming from businesses, research institutes and commercial organisations, by participating in the system architecture, or transfer and internationalisation teams, assist the boards in developing and implementing concrete activities.

The management is also involved in the internationalisation process of the cluster. The international co-operation encompasses, among others, the recent initiative—it's OWL-EA ('European Alliance for the Securing of the Top Position in Intelligent Technical Systems'). Funded by the Federal Ministry of Education and Research, it aims at developing a co-operation model with the Canadian region, British Columbia. As a practically oriented and industry-driven initiative, it should lead to the unlocking of more innovation potential for SMEs. Another example of international 'cluster-to-cluster' (C2C) co-operation is the partnership with Finnish cluster, DIMMEC. The objective of this merger of interests is the development of inter-disciplinary, cross-industry solutions, in the field of digitisation and production, with the intent of time-to-market and development time reduction. Such a partnership fits into the German government strategy, which aims to support the smart manufacturing, by strengthening the regional competence centres and clusters and their targeted internationalisation, and in consequence, their international competition. Besides, it's OWL has been developing constructive links with China and Turkey.

Some sceptical opinions are questioning the importance of the institutional framework and reducing them, mainly, to some marketing related activities. Although the management focuses on various dimensions of cluster functioning, such as technology and R&D strategy, operational aspects, including internationalisation and marketing, are crucial for creating the brand and increasing its visibility. Governance structure is critical, as it can guarantee the value-added for all shareholders. Cluster management is perceived in terms of balancing stakeholders' rights and orchestrating various cluster activities. It enjoys a strong mandate and is allowed to speak on behalf of all CCs. This legitimacy facilitates carrying out negotiations and representing the cluster outside. Hence, it soothes the way for decision-making. Conversely, it confers the legitimacy on SMEs, which is critical, given the liability of smallness experienced in their external relations. The board consisting of major companies' representatives is a powerful body making decisions and contributing substantially to the cluster development. Thus, the governance structure is seen as a critical factor, enabling smooth and efficient operation of the cluster.

Summing up, this section of the analysis, it is worth stressing that despite some scepticism, the institutional framework may rise, as the formal governance structures and management of cluster play an essential role in its functioning and, in particular, in light of challenges related to the I4.0. The formal institutional setting, as the example of it's OWL may show, has been regarded since the beginning with some doubts, if not criticism. Nevertheless, it has proved crucial for the technology transfer, organising projects, developing marketing, branding of the cluster, initiating foreign co-operation, seeking partners abroad or attracting talents. Also, local firms have, over time, become more and more convinced of the benefits of it's OWL brand. The distinctions and awards are additional proofs of the high quality of management. In times of re-industrialisation, the institutional framework in clusters should focus on the provision of (semi)public goods. It should ascertain the ICs (category of cluster commons, as suggested by Sölvell, 2015), i.e. the capabilities supporting the innovativeness across industries.

4 Developing a Conceptual Model

As inferred from the in-depth, semi-structured interviews held in 2018, in Paderborn and Lemgo, with CRs (managers and scholars anonymised as E1–E7), there is some general agreement among them, as to the importance of individual factors for the success of it's OWL. Firstly, 'knowledge is there, and it is a must for any I4.0 cluster' (E1). Secondly, agglomeration of business and industry is also critical, as well as the presence of business partners (B2B), and supply and demand in place, are seen as a given asset of the cluster. The institutional dimension, although, perceived sceptically at the beginning, becomes, over time, an advantage. It is now recognised as a basic framework, which helps to leverage the expertise and competences, to develop trust among companies and to reinforce positive attitudes. In other words, it's OWL by combining the three pillars mentioned above—a set of critical attributes— can stimulate the advancement in business digital transformation—in I4.0. As seen by it's OWL representatives, cluster-I4.0 relation is not a 'one-way street'. Not only clusters contribute to the development of I4.0, but it goes both ways—I4.0 or digitisation shape clusters, as well.

International Relations and Openness

According to it's OWL members, there is a clear need to open up the cluster, of more international co-operation, which reinforces the local base of competencies and inversely contributes to local knowledge (Fredin, Miörner & Jogmark, 2019). Cluster openness remains a critical factor. As stressed by it's OWL representatives (E4), responsible for internationalisation, 'generally, it is always crucial to keep one's eyes open to what is happening globally. Increasing international visibility and extending one's global network only works, if one is aware of a global picture. In this way, the cluster internationalises'. It's OWL has a clear brand that is recognised by its unique character, namely the clustering of companies, universities, research institutes and other organisations in the OWL region, which has an evident culture of co-operation. By working closely with other national and international technology regions and clusters, it's OWL helps establish OWL as a centre for cutting-edge technology. Successful collaboration enhances the performance of the Leading-Edge Cluster, increases the visibility of the OWL region worldwide, and at the same time, expands the network of cluster partners. The internationalisation of cluster typically equals the internationalisation of its members, as well. 'So, it's OWL as a brand internationalises, but through the cluster's efforts to engage in internationalisation, the partners become more international as well, because they are a part of the cluster and are involved in certain activities' (E4). Events such as delegation visits, fairs, participation in international workshops, all support the internationalisation of it's OWL as such, and of its members. However, attracting companies from outside, specifically the foreign direct investors (FDI), to the Leading-Edge Cluster, has not been practised.

Various channels of internationalisation are applied by it's OWL, but not all are possible. Interestingly, the R&D collaboration and subsequently, the exchange of knowledge and transfer of technologies, becomes the critical aspect and component of this co-operation. This aspect of the activity is encouraged and supported by it's OWL-dedicated internationalisation team. Other commercial activities, mainly exporting, happen as the initiatives of firms, themselves. It reflects on some trends and purposeful actions undertaken by the federal government, within the High-Tech Strategy Internationalisation of Leading-Edge Clusters, Forward-Looking Projects, and Comparable Networks (Clusters-Networks-International, www.bmbf.de/en/internationalisation-of-leading-edge-clusters-forward-looking-projects-and-comparable-1416.html). 'Sharing our own abilities with others and extending them with international knowledge, will help us stay competitive and innovative in future' (E4). Strengthening the international networking of research and industry is therefore, critical. As it has been argued, new promising technologies, products and solutions arise through co-operation across different sectors and technologies. Potential foreign co-operation partners should have complementary competencies, compared to the German partner cluster, their management organisation or proper structure, as well as the objective to design joint rules of co-operation. The promoted formula of internationalisation of cluster appears to deviate from the established and typical approach. Namely, under the notion of cluster internationalisation, what is meant is mainly the support of cluster organisations (COs) to SMEs and the assistance in their foreign expansion, primarily in the form of export. It's OWL's internationalisation is, however, considered as leveraging the complementarities with foreign partner clusters. It materialises via subsequent exchange of knowledge and technology transfer, while creating synergies to advance the innovations.

Internationalisation is seen as a way of improving available local competences, to enable the reinforcement of the local knowledge. Partner clusters
should be selected, based on their capabilities as someone to 'learn from'.
Building on the culture of co-operation, inherent in the OWL region, the
diagnosed complementarities with foreign partners, must create the funda-
mentals for collaboration, aiming to increase the joint chances to win the
international global competition in the area of I4.0. Internationalisation is
the way to achieve a particular aim, and not necessarily an objective, in
itself. It is supposed to help to gain valuable knowledge from outside and
leverage it for the benefit of it's OWL, as well as prevent possible dangerous inertia or lock-in of the cluster. It is a pre-requisite for maintaining
competitiveness and for providing constituent firms with access to foreign
'know-how' (Turkina & Van Assche, 2018). The ultimate goal of the cluster
is to contribute to regional development, create jobs and further improve the
regional wealth and prosperity.

So, the cluster is internationally oriented, but it does not seem justified to
speak about the clear *hubbing* (geographic expansion) of the cluster concept. 'It is natural for companies, for universities and for research institutes to internationalise, given a globalised world' (E4). Thus, in the case
of it's OWL, 'the cluster concept is not stretching as such, but there is a
strong international orientation. This comes with globalisation and the
need to constantly acquire new knowledge' (E4). Nevertheless, as seen in
it's OWL, some *stretching* of the cluster is happening already, but it is an
evolutionary process. *Blending* (sectoral expansion) but mainly *hubbing*,
namely, increasing the geographical scale, both prove essential for the
upgrading of the cluster competences, as the option to learn from others. It
should be considered as a step preventing in the long run possible cluster
decline. Opinions on this topic are, however, not unanimous. 'Stretching is
not something really positive and should not be seen as an aim in itself. It
happens anyway, but should be regarded as a natural stage for the upgrading of cluster competences. Opening to the outside brings fresh air, new
impetus, prevents the lock-in of cluster, and ultimately, it helps to tackle
challenges of megatrends like Industry 4.0. The cluster should combine two
types of membership—close, full of those located here, and some associated members co-operating more loosely. Remaining flexible is important'
(E1). Proximity and geographical co-location should remain a central feature of the cluster. 'Stretching is something positive, as long as it provides
more options of learning and helps to sustain the competitive advantage,
which is a "sine qua non" condition for upgrading local skills and expertise,
for staying in the top cluster globally, and avoiding risks of degradation'
(E3). It can be surmised that clusters would change under the pressure of
digitisation. They would need to remain open geographically, and be more

diversified sectorally, but these processes should be seen, in fact, as a way of bolstering the core established competencies; as a necessary upgrading of local knowledge.

Cluster Importance for Small and Medium Enterprises

Clusters play a particularly critical role for SMEs. They are the backbone of the regional economy also affected by digitisation, yet often incapable of adopting new technologies, launching new solutions and following the suits of larger firms. What is central for cluster management are initiatives aimed at transferring the 'know-how' and technology to SMEs and micro-firms. Although, experts point out the need to cater to those clusters (and its members) with revealed potential, i.e. those who have already passed the market test, and proved they would be self-sustained in the long run, once the triggering of initial funding expires. Start-ups cannot be ordered from the top, created from scratch or commissioned by someone, so, clusters should also develop from natural bottom-up processes and natural accumulation of a critical mass of firms.

In the eyes of it's OWL representatives, the presence of customers in the region (i.e. the business-to-business relations, B2B) proves critical for cluster development. Many manufacturing firms are here. These are HCs, often family-run, only slightly exceeding the threshold of being defined as a large firm. Its owners still regard some as small start-ups, although, in manufacturing, this scalability is a critical factor of competitiveness. Thus, the internal scale economies, which are missing at the firm's level, must be compensated by the cluster externalities, i.e. agglomeration positive effects and spill-overs.

It's OWL hosts diversified, yet supplementary industries, such as mechanical engineering, automotive supply and electrical engineering, which is evidence of specific technological relatedness or a locally provided RV. The range of successfully completed transfer projects, and the variety of industries represented, can confirm this (Figure 4.1).

Intelligent technical systems, which constitutes the core competence of it's OWL, is a cross-sectoral, horizontal issue, linking various stakeholders along the value chain. This RV also helps in a way, as firms which are not direct competitors, are more willing to co-operate. Instant collaboration across established domains, industries and groups of stakeholders seems 'a must' these days. As argued, therefore, businesses need to master crossover innovation, for instance, by the re-combination of old ideas in new ways (Cooke, 2018).

As seen in it's OWL, (E2) 'the related variety of the cluster is achieved through the higher-level topic of mechatronics. It means a merger of

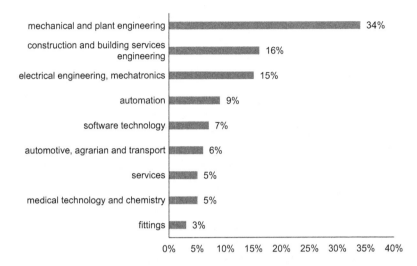

Figure 4.1 Distribution of companies according to the industry—73 focused completed transfer projects (July 1, 2014 to June 30, 2016)

Source: Own elaboration based on data courtesy of the representative of it's OWL Clustermanagement GmbH, 2018, www.its-owl.com/fileadmin/PDF/Informationsmaterialien/2017-Technology_Transfer_web.pdf

mechanical, electrical, control engineering and informatics. Furthermore, mechatronics is also a superior domain of automation'. Thus, by its very nature, the mechatronics and the SE, which is the core of it's OWL cluster, seems to incorporate the idea of RV.

The strategy of it's OWL development assumes setting up new student programmes, designing new syllabuses, creating new research institutes and further developing technologies. Path dependency is visible in the history of this region, as well. The origins of it's OWL go back to Heinz Nixdorf and his pioneering work on merging the IT and engineering, which, at that time, was a complete novelty. Today, this fusion of IT-Engineering seems to best depict the realms of I4.0. Innovation projects—bilateral initiatives between large firms and research institutions—result in generating new knowledge and new technologies. It proves extremely important to make it available to other local firms. This results in the idea of 'taking these best practices—technologies—out of selected bilateral projects (literally—extracting out of the brackets as some common element) and transferring them to other firms' (E5). It has happened, however, in a very informal and non-institutionalised way. People are carriers of this 'know-how'. It's OWL management has been considering setting up some digital online platform to network better the people who are carrying this unique expertise and the outcome of the projects. Although, for the time being, there is no proper physical/online repository. This knowledge is still sticky, tacit, not codified or stored in any library or archives.

Work 4.0, entrepreneurship, transfer of technology and innovations remain four pillars of it's OWL strategy. Special attention is being paid to the entrepreneurship of existing firms. The aim is consequently, not only to help to create new start-ups, but also to assist those already active, old, often a family-run business. The availability of smart factories, for instance, something most SMEs would not have afforded, is one such initiative. Assistance is provided by technology scouting or developing new business models. Interestingly, large firms who develop certain technologies themselves are willing to share this knowledge. They set up academia and offer specific courses. In that way, a 'win-win' situation is created. SMEs can get access to valuable new technologies; large firms can train future co-workers.

Local companies also appreciate marketing actions, which increase cluster visibility. Firms are identifying themselves with the brand of it's OWL (E1, E3 and E4). 'Often, when they go somewhere and take part in fairs or exhibitions, they take rollups, and represent proudly, it's OWL'. 'The brand over the last five years, has indeed proved to be valuable for firms. It helps in contacts with outsiders, is seen as a certificate of high quality and expertise, (Kompetenz Vermutung) and helps attract talents'. Co-ordinated actions help, but proximity, trust, and frequent contacts, all matter a lot for successful development of ITSs, and ultimately, for the cluster's growth. The initial funding won in the competition from BMBF has already expired. Following the rounds of negotiations, it has been replaced with assistance from the federal government of North Rhine-Westphalia (NRW) to the tune of 56 million EUR (must be doubled with money from the business). In 2015, the regional government of NRW secured the additional funding of 930,000 euro for it's OWL (www.land.nrw/de/pressemitteilung/land-foerdert-spitzencluster-its-owl-mit-930000-euro). With support from the state of NRW, the activities of it's OWL will be continued from 2018 to 2022 (www.hni.uni-paderborn.de/en/research/priority-projects-in-research/leading-edge-cluster-its-owl/). Overall, with the support of state, federal and EU governments, projects of around EUR 200 million are to be implemented up till 2022 (Who makes SMEs . . . , 2019).

The need for developing technology, but even more so the role of proper and efficient transferring of it can be regarded in terms of ICs; as a provision of much needed capabilities crucial for innovativeness. Regions need ICs, which act as a pool of idiosyncratic regional assets, enabling innovation processes and enhancing development paths (Pisano & Shih, 2012; Bailey & de Propris, 2014).

Contrary to simple assumptions and despite some impressive advancements through ICT, knowledge is not a cost-free commodity, but subject to path dependency and innovation is spatially concentrated and strongly supported by a specific, idiosyncratic, systemic context (Bramanti, 2016). It is of paramount importance for SMEs who cannot afford many new technologies, lack funding, can be under-staffed and suffer the liability of smallness (Aldrich & Auster, 1986). Cluster SMEs can capitalise on different inter-firm collaborations within clusters to enhance the growth in the face of various constraints deriving from the size liability (Kale & Arditi, 1998; Hessels & Parker, 2013). A crucial role for SMEs in the OWL region is played, in this respect, by the smart factory—a laboratory where they can see the practical application of new solutions. ICs are co-developed and shaped by interactions between technology providers (supply) and technology beneficiaries—SMEs (demand). The SmartFactoryOWL from Fraunhofer Society and the OWL University of Applied Sciences, located in Lemgo, is a manufacturer-independent I4.0 application and demonstration centre, and also a testing area for the SME sector. Interested companies can try out and test new I4.0 technologies, and then integrate them into their production and work processes with the support of experts. The key competencies provided encompass image processing and pattern recognition, or analytical methods in automation. Besides, firms can benefit from services, such as demonstration models, consulting or training. The provision of such commons also happens via other establishments. HMI Transfer Laboratory is the Bielefeld-located human-machine interaction transfer laboratory operated jointly by Bielefeld University, research institutes, such as Heinz Nixdorf Institute in Paderborn, the Institute for Cognition and Robotics (CoR-Lab) and the CITEC. Provided competencies include virtual/augmented reality, interactive robotics, machine learning and automatic image processing, whereas the available services encompass pilot projects, demonstration models, consulting and training. Another example is Paderborn-based Systems Engineering Live LAB, associated with the Fraunhofer IEM. It is an application and transfer centre, in which the latest methods and tools for the development of technical systems are tested, compared and employed. Companies can learn about SE techniques and languages, model-based systems, engineering and are provided with assistance in pilot projects, consulting, training or certifications. The practice of the cluster functioning re-directs the attention and re-focus to the concept of ICs, to the need of not only assuring the provision, but also the dissemination and broader availability of new technologies and competences.

Related variety seems to be another crucial component emanating from the review of cluster activities, and the discussions and exchange of opinions of experts. In it's OWL cluster, it takes the form of SE, i.e. the efforts to merge various engineering fields which is a pre-requisite for successful implementation of I4.0. SE encompasses inter-disciplinary engineering and engineering management that focus on the design and execution of very complex systems throughout the whole life cycle. It combines social, human with technical disciplines and handles issues, such as risk management or optimisation. SE is about discovery and problem-solving, meaning that the need for cross-fertilisation and marrying disciplines cannot be under-estimated (Suwala & Micek, 2018) and inter-disciplinary integration seems critical. It, among others, is the task of Fraunhofer Institute, IEM, or HeinzNixdorf Institute at the University of Paderborn, (www. hni.uni-paderborn.de/en/research/priority-projects-in-research/leading-edge-cluster-its-owl/). SE meets the requirements of developing modern, extremely complex, production systems. The continuous discipline-spanning approach (system modelling and analysis) enables the development of multi-disciplinary systems. SE offers a holistic and inter-disciplinary, hence an appropriate, perspective for analysing I4.0 in the modern business environment, as it focuses on design, development and implementation of complex systems (Bureš, 2018). SE ensures that all possible project or system dimensions are considered and integrated into a whole. It requires the incorporation of various aspects of complex systems and processes, and contribution from diverse technical disciplines. So, it might be argued, it stipulates the growing importance of the provision of ICs and foresees the role of RV, inevitably. The 'V' model, central in SE (developed in the space industry in the 80s), assumes the joint work on given problems or concepts. It happens first, separately, by each domain (e.g. mechanical engineering, software development and electrical engineering), and then by the integration phase, when all the solutions proposed independently, should be bound together. (E2) 'Some joint syntax, operating the same model vocabulary, is necessary for effective communication among different engineering fields'. The attributes of I4.0 and the challenges it poses for manufacturing, in fact, intelligent technical production systems, require a certain level of this inter-engineering collaboration.

The RV and diversification imply certain industrial and sectoral openness and a readiness to accept less specialisation. The peculiarities of mechatronics and SE (i.e. the core of it's OWL) suggest some cluster's *stretching*. In particular, they facilitate its *blending*, i.e. the expansion of subjects, areas, if not sectors. *Stretching* of the cluster, as seen by it's OWL representatives, though it is perhaps inevitable, should be kept to the minimum. Otherwise, the core feature and idiosyncrasy of the term 'cluster' might be missed. Therefore, geographic expanding can be accepted to some limited extent, likewise increasing the scope of primary industries. Clusters, nevertheless, should stay focused on their core competences, on a few related domains, such as mechanical engineering, electrical/electronic and automotive supply industries.

Provision of ICs, RV and Stretching Processes in It's OWL

In it's OWL cluster, the ICs can be associated with the idea of technology transfer, and in particular, the existence of smart factory. RV, on the other hand, materialises via work on SE, which implies the fusion of mechanical engineering, IT, software engineering and others. Based on the results of it's OWL field study, it might be argued that the clusters' relevance for I4.0 development would rest on the provision of ICs, i.e. manufacturing and technology capabilities supporting the innovativeness across industries, and on the emergence of RV, i.e. the externalities of co-location of different industries sharing some commonalities (Figure 4.2).

The importance of ICs would be the more articulated, the larger the share of SMEs' inhibiting clusters. These firms are usually considered as poorer—equipped to face technological challenges than large companies, which can afford more risk-taking and have funds and staff to handle the digital transformation. They are affected by the liability of smallness, which makes the provision of ICs even more critical (Figure 4.3).

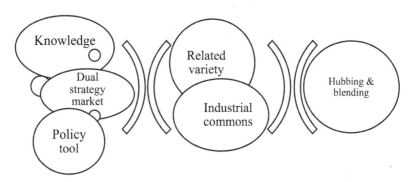

Figure 4.2 Building blocks of the conceptual model for studying Industry 4.0 clusters
Source: Author's own proposal

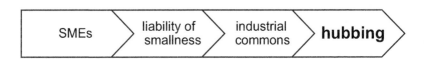

Figure 4.3 Roots of the importance of *industrial commons*
Source: Author's own proposal

Related variety, on the other hand, can be linked to the idiosyncrasy of I4.0, namely, the SE underpinning it. SE promotes a holistic and inter-disciplinary approach, which is crucial for the development of complex products and processes, such as ITSs—a backbone of I4.0.

It's OWL centred around the field of mechatronics and SE, which are characterised by a holistic and inter-disciplinary perspective, incorporating various engineering and manufacturing areas, implies the importance of RV. This, in consequence, justifies some *blending* of the cluster, i.e. it calls for some reaching out to other areas, or a spreading of core competencies to other familiar fields (Figure 4.4). On the other hand, the dominance of medium-sized firms, in need of accessing ICs, seems to warrant some processes of *hubbing* of the cluster. The optimal properly designed geographical expansion should enable tapping into external skills, competences and technologies, and subsequently, allow the upgrading of it's OWL's existing excellences.

As the case of a leading-edge cluster t's OWL demonstrates, the co-existence of suppliers and customers in the region (incarnating, in fact, the dual strategy) proves critical seed for developing more institutionalised cluster. A complementary essential factor turns out to be knowledge—technologies and know-how rooted in the region—its universities and research institutions, such as Fraunhofer Institutes. These two were at the bottom of any further development of a proper cluster—a backbone for subsequent initiatives. Adding the institutional layer, i.e. the policy component was regarded as a complementary step, buttressing what has been already achieved to galvanise it to the benefits of the whole region further. These factors can be considered as crucial for successful implementation of digitisation in the area. Yet, the I4.0 adoption affects the cluster, conversely. It creates the need for developing ICs, i.e. forces local stakeholders to provide capabilities inevitable for further prosperous growth. I4.0 by its very nature abolishes borders and boundaries among firms and sectors facilitating cross-sectoral approach and encourages the development of RVs—of complementary, but diversified competences. Thus, I4.0 reshapes the essence of local cluster and forces it into some modification. It requires incorporating a more inter-sectoral systemic approach, focusing on the provision of ICs and the emergence of RVs. Among others, it facilitates the processes of opening—of increasing

Figure 4.4 Roots of importance of *related variety*

Source: Author's own proposal

both the geographical scale and industrial scope. This *stretching*—including *hubbing* and *blending*—further reinforces the original knowledge base, as it prevents inertia and allows for learning options. The institutional layer of the cluster and marketing activities, which enable the reaching out of the cluster, plays a unique role and should not be under-estimated (Figure 4.5).

The conceptual model, proposed below, refers to the new concept of 'the open region' by Schmidt, Müller, Ibert and Brinks (2018), which offers a heuristic view on a proactive policy, allowing for the dialectic interplay between territorial openness and closure, and aiming at exploiting opportunities for regions' innovation by mobilising external expertise. It's OWL is an industry-led cluster, where the top results from research institutions build the technology platform, to which industry partners can have access. Transfer projects enable SME's to benefit, significantly, from innovation, and progressive governance organisation co-exists with a considerable commitment of industry partners (steering board and advisory board). To achieve its long-term goals and jointly manage the challenges of digitalisation, it's OWL forms new national and international partnerships with partners, who have complementary skills and proven track records in related areas (concept based on strength). It would appear that, based on it's OWL representatives' opinions, knowledge matters most for the advancement of I4.0 in the cluster: 'the fact that people know the subject, speak the same technical language, the cognitive proximity and favourable environment for generating and disseminating innovations is critical. Next or parallel comes the business aspect—co-location of related industries, co-operation and competition among local firms and the presence of customers. Finally, as perhaps one of its slightly less important features—the institutional umbrella aspect' (E2). The cluster's role in facilitating the digital business transformation in the region can be summarised by saying that it serves as a platform, which allows the partners to work jointly across all disciplines and along the entire value chain.

The first part of this study—it's OWL case research yielded the conceptual framework, which might be harnessed for analysing the I4.0 clusters. It is a broad and general scaffolding, which might be further developed and enriched. However, already, the explorative study has shown just how critical is the role played by the provision of ICs. What is worth stressing even more is the relevance of assuring the availability of these capabilities, and in turn, the importance of technology transfer. It has also demonstrated the importance of RV, without, however, discussing the exact externalities stemming from such co-existence of diversified yet complementary sectors and benefits, accruing to this range of various industries. The sections below outline in more details the four key concepts identified in the first part of the research.

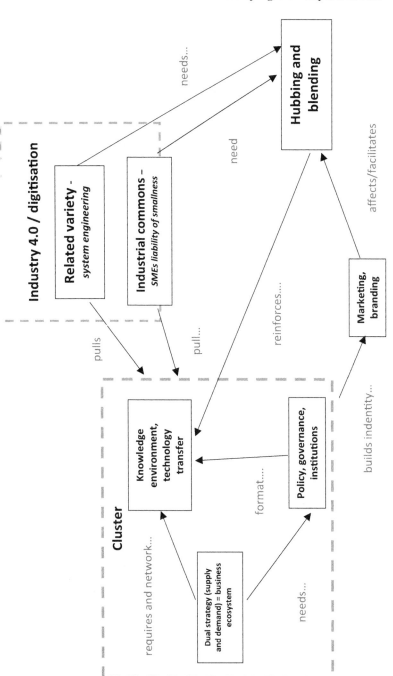

Figure 4.5 Evolution of cluster in the Industry 4.0 era

Source: Author's own proposal

Industrial Commons

Industrial commons might be regarded as a specific category of cluster commons. These according to Sölvell (2015) could be understood as a meeting place, paths and bridges, which facilitate the spill-overs among cluster members (Morgulis-Yakushev & Sölvell, 2017). One can think of these commons as the 'white spaces' in between the actors (Sölvell & Williams, 2013). Commons are not limited to existing, already available components, but can be designed, created, constructed or even transferred from outside.

Pisano and Shih (2009) define ICs as encompassing knowledge, competences, skills, labour market, equipment, institutions and the broader R&D environment; as a bundle of regional and industry idiosyncratic assets, often constituting a kind of public good. Being the backbone for innovation and competitiveness, they are not only embedded in firms and scientific institutions, but also geographically rooted. Regions need ICs (perceived as a pool of idiosyncratic regional assets enabling innovation processes) to attract investors, to retain business, to prevent re-location and also to reverse the trend of offshoring (Pisano & Shih, 2012; Bailey & de Propris, 2014). ICs as shared supply chains and knowledge bases (Buciuni & Pisano, 2015) are critical for regional development.

Results of Cohendet, Grandadam, Mehouachi and Simon's (2018) study reveal that local commons are composed of both a pool of resources (scientific knowledge, artistic talents, financial support, infrastructure, etc.) and a dense middle ground. The latter is understood as common cognitive mechanisms, such as spaces, projects and events, that serve as the liaison between the underground and the upper ground. The pool of resources and the middle ground not only co-exist, but they can also enrich each other mutually, as the middle ground contributes to an increase of the resources pool, which in turn, can upgrade the quality of middle ground connections.

Despite some impressive advancements, thanks to ICT, which enables distant communication and collaboration, knowledge is not a free commodity, but subject to path dependency, and innovation is usually spatially concentrated and contingent to specific, idiosyncratic context (Bramanti, 2016). So, any activity based on advanced knowledge must be accompanied by some bundles of public goods and services, and the existence of the ICs. We can conclude here that the concept of IC draws on the triple helix idea purporting clusters, which assumes the co-existence of academia, administration and industry, as a pre-requisite for fruitful cluster developments.

According to Barzotto and Mariotti (2018), ICs or external economies of localisation comprise a skilled workforce, supply networks, manufacturing culture and social capital, which are necessary to support manufacturing. ICs can be used as an appropriate description of the resources available in district areas (Barzotto, Corò & Volpe, 2017). They can be classified as goods, whose use is difficult to exclude from potential beneficiaries and characterised by some rivalry, especially when allocations of these resources fall below a critical threshold. They are seen as a positive externality and some public good, implying that a company might draw on the assets of the local commons without payment and property rights.

IC, defined in terms of a knowledge base and its mechanisms, knowledge ecosystem composition, as well as its volatility/stability, play a critical role in knowledge—intense clusters (Květoň & Kadlec, 2018). However, IC in the region is not just about the knowledge, but also about the local business. Hidalgo (2015, p. 142) stresses the interdependence between local industries and local know-how, arguing that 'knowledge needs the presence of industries, as much as industries need the presence of knowledge and know-how'.

Untraded interdependencies, pertaining to clusters and making them attractive locations draw on knowledge spill-overs (Vicente, 2018). This crucial production factor can be desired in terms of only 'having access to' or 'appropriating it'. Favouring appropriation usually results in sparsely linked clusters, whereas denser relations develop as a consequence of an 'accessibility approach'. These strategies, in turn, draw on the types of proximity featuring in a given cluster, whether only geographical (distance) or also an organisational and institutional one, i.e. social relations and conventional institutions (Vicente, 2018). IC and, in particular, a knowledge ecosystem as the primary component are contingent on the revealed proximity among the cluster members (physical, institutional, cultural, etc.) and the strategy adopted (to share or to own). Likewise, the perception of IC and its importance is modulated by various factors and is not automatic (Perry, 2007; Lechner & Leyronas, 2012). It can further interact outside the cluster in multiple formats—be explored, integrated or exploited.

Morgulis-Yakushev and Sölvell (2017), argue that the depth of the ties between cluster members can be enhanced through various types of 'bridge-building' activities. It remains noteworthy; however, how bridge-building actions lead to any real 'traffic' (measured as activities on the bridges), and how this traffic relates to firm's performance. The 'bridges' include meeting points, organised fora, project platforms and networking events, cluster breakfasts, pub evenings and the like (Morgulis-Yakushev & Sölvell, 2017). Engel (2014) suggests regarding *the commons* as shared gifts.

Related Variety

Drawing on Malmberg and Power (2006), a 'true' cluster can be defined as a spatially bounded agglomeration of related activities, which is based on co-opetition with actors sharing a feeling of belonging. The concept of RV is understood as the relatedness of a knowledge base utilised by different sectors within a region and can indeed be regarded as a critical factor of a cluster's development (Gaschet et al., 2017). The concept of RV was initially put forward by Frenken, Van Oort and Verburg (2007). There is a growing perception of regional clusters as an incarnation of specialisation in an array of related industries, not necessarily specialisation in a narrowly defined single industry (Delgado, Porter & Stern, 2016). The importance of RV may also be interpreted as a recognition of a growing tendency to replace the economies of scale with economies of scope, which is happening thanks to the I4.0.

Related variety is a concept known in evolutionary economic geography, which sees relations between knowledge spill-overs and economic growth, development or renewal (Asheim, Boschma & Cooke, 2011; Boschma & Iammarino, 2007). It refers to the variety of industries present, within a given region, that are linked cognitively (Frenken, Van Oort & Verburg, 2007). These are believed to be able to better leverage the potential for learning and growth, and to give impetus to the emergence of new industries (Boschma, 2014). Inter-industry diversity and technological complementarities are crucial for the development of innovations (Mudambi & Swift, 2012). It implies that new, value-creating innovations are more likely to arise at the intersections of technologies, and these advantages are based on the presence of diverse knowledge bases (Mudambi, Narula & Santangelo, 2018).

Related variety means that the region's different industries have some commonalities enabling knowledge exchange and spill-overs. RV stands for learning, which is focused on the context-specific intangible assets available in the region. It demonstrates that regional specialisations and knowledge bases offer opportunities for future diversification, also by linking together different industries or areas of expertise (Boschma, 2014; Frenken, Van Oort & Verburg, 2007).

The advent of computerised manufacturing technologies marks a clear departure from the logic of the previous economic era, in which the growing complexity of technologies required more specialisation, resulting in modularisation of technologies and fragmentation of value chains (Alcácer et al., 2016; Langlois, 2002). Currently, advanced production technologies allow the consolidating of subsequent phases of manufacturing processes and more integral product architecture with closer co-ordination of activities (Rezk, Srai &Williamson, 2016).

Related variety might be summarised as dynamic and complementary externalities originating in similar industries. Aarstad, Kvitastein and Jakobsen (2016) define it as the deployment of additional factor inputs, in contrast to specialisation seen as economies of scale, and in terms of local competition. RV can also be associated with technological diversification and knowledge spill-overs, occurring among firms operating in 'different but related' sectors (Cainelli & Ganau, 2019). Gaschet et al. (2017) mention the relatedness of knowledge bases, used by different sectors within a region. RV implies the existence of 'knowledge platforms', which organises the re-combination of technologies in overlapping industries. In this light, the cluster can be seen as a 'geographic concentration of linked industries' (Gaschet et al., 2017), and available studies confirm the role of RV as a success driver, particularly for the most significant European clusters.

The extent to which companies are linked to each other improves their innovativeness, whereas the diversity of knowledge distributed among them, offers the variety that strengthens regional resilience (Sedita, de Noni & Pilotti, 2015; Fratesi & Rodriguez-Pose, 2016). RV is rooted in the existing regional knowledge base and encompasses two complementary dimensions of external knowledge flows: 'cognitive proximity' and local 'absorptive capacity', which might contribute to a region's development (Bramanti, 2016). As neither pure specialisation nor sole diversification can promise regional success, the exploitation of RV has been advocated as the right way forward. Indeed, the concept of RV stresses that knowledge between the actors should not be *too* dissimilar and implies that sectors are complementary in terms of competences (Boschma & Iammarino, 2009).

The concept of *RV* was introduced in an attempt to resolve an earlier empirical question put forward by Glaeser, Kallal, Scheinkman and Shleifer (1992), whether regions benefit most from being specialised or being diversified. This 'controversy' is commonly referred to as 'MAR versus Jacobs'. It depicts the tensions between the Marshall, Arrow and Romer theories, which suggested that spill-overs take place primarily within a single industry, and the Jacobs' theory (1969, p. 59) stating that 'the greater the sheer numbers and varieties of divisions of labour already achieved in an economy, the greater the economy's inherent capacity for adding still more kinds of goods and services'.

RV seems to be closely associated with the concept of smart specialisation (or 3S smart specialisation strategy—Koschatzky, Kroll, Schnabl & Stahlecker, 2017). As proposed by McCann & Ortega-Argilés (2014), smart specialisation, while being an explicit focus of regional policy, nevertheless, draws on the relatedness concept. It argues that diversifying into related industries improves the robustness and resilience of the local economy. Consequently, the economic growth of the region can be stimulated by the technological diversification of its embedded industries (Elekes, Boschma, & Lengyel 2019). Smart specialisation strategies are often perceived as recycled cluster strategies (Valdaliso, Magro, Navarro, Jose Aranguren & Wilson, 2014), and recently, have become more critically regarded (Hassink & Gong, 2019).

Based on the analysis of Norwegian regions, Aarstad, Kvitastein and Jakobsen (2016) showed that RV is a positive driver of enterprise innovation, whereas the opposite can be said about *unrelated variety*. Thus, regions representing simultaneously high levels of RV and low levels of *unrelated variety* can optimise enterprise performance. Also, results obtained by Gaschet et al. (2017) confirm the role played by RV in the successful development of European photonics clusters. As neither too much specialisation nor too much diversification is good, the concept of variety seems to offer a promising middle ground. Whereas, the *unrelated variety*, understood as a pool of assets accumulated in a particular region, can be perceived as a static category stressing the separateness; the RV, drawing on Jacob's externalities, should be explained as a dynamic concept emphasising complementarities.

The measure of RV is usually based on the hierarchical structure of official industry classifications (e.g. NACE). It is assumed that the more digits two industries share in the formal industrial classification, the more closely related they must be. Thus, classification-based relatedness is usually presented by reference to the number of initial digits these industries have in common. There are alternative measures, which include, for instance, information about the export portfolio, firm offer portfolio or shared inputs. These are much less common, but there is a growing awareness that frequently used relatedness measures, based on industry classification, might be not reflecting all relatedness ties (Firgo & Mayerhofer, 2018; Kuusk & Martynovich, 2018). RV builds on the application of relatedness linkages, which as proved by Kuusk and Martynovich (2018), could change over time and have a 'best before date'. The findings obtained can support previous claims stressing the dynamic nature of relatedness and give rise to the doubts of how accurately we can capture it. Issues such as stability, age or symmetry of these ties are additional aspects of RV, which deserve attention along with its dynamic. These dimensions seem to be captured in this volume by reference to the *blending* processes.

Fitjar and Timmermans (2019) demonstrate that relatedness comes with some costs, in terms of increased labour market competition. Based on the case of the Norwegian petroleum industry, they proved that the risk of de-skilling in related industries might outweigh potential knowledge spill-over benefits from their relatedness to the petroleum industry. Consequently, relatedness seems to have its losers and winners.

Vicente (2018) argues that the growing need for more cross-industrial approach requires more co-operation between actors with heterogeneous knowledge bases and the creation of markets spanning the standard industrial classifications. Against this background, clusters may represent, not only the answer to the multi-faceted need for new knowledge combinations, but also offer a smoother transition to new transversal innovation systems (Cooke, 2012). The need to focus on RV, rather than purely sectoral narrow specialisation in cluster exploration, may also embody the fact that agglomeration forces may operate at the capability level, rather than at the industry level (Buciuni & Pisano, 2015). The proper assessment of relatedness is complicated by the increasing relevance of transversal technologies, i.e. technologies that are developed and applied in slightly different sectors (Giannini, Iacobucci & Perugini, 2019). Technological relatedness guarantees, on the one hand, a level of similarity, which enables the exchange of knowledge and efficient learning, but on the other—a certain cognitive distance allowing for new knowledge combinations and innovations (Dohse, Fornahl & Vehrke, 2018). It can lead to some path dependencies in technology development but should prevent a dangerous lock-in in the long run (Hassink, 2016).

To stimulate cluster heterogeneity and to avoid the risk of becoming too narrowly focused, its thematic boundary should be opened and related knowledge from inside, added. Alternatively, the geographic borders should become permeable, allowing the sourcing of knowledge from different locations (Fornahl & Hassink, 2017); it includes going international. International expansion offers access to complementary assets and enables the establishment of new market relationships and sourcing information, which may not be available in the domestic market (Morisson, Rabellotti & Zirulia, 2013). Thus, it can enrich the cluster's knowledge base and make it more heterogeneous (Bathelt, Malmberg & Maskell, 2004). The inflow of mixed knowledge, in turn, can lead to a revitalisation and renewal of the cluster, acting as a positive shock. Internationalisation can thus be considered as a channel to increase heterogeneity and infuse new ideas into a region. As a result, this volume also investigates the concept of cluster expansion, not only understood as internationalisation (Osarenkhoe & Fjellström, 2017; Islankina & Thurner, 2018), but in terms of *stretching* processes.

Stretching—Blending and Hubbing

The cluster has already expanded from its original concept and, in consequence, a *stretching* of the definition has occurred, resulting in growing detachment from Porter's concept (Desrochers & Sautet, 2004; Fløysand, Jakobsen & Bjarnar, 2012; Malmberg & Power, 2006; Martin & Sunley, 2003; Tödtling & Trippl, 2005). *Stretching* can materialise via *hubbing*, i.e. expansion in geographical scale, and *blending*, i.e. expansion in industrial scope (Njøs et al., 2017a).

It is likely that *stretching* processes might be further compounded by the implications of the fourth industrial revolution (Götz & Jankowska, 2017).

The twin strategies of *hubbing* and *blending* (i.e. expanding geographically and sectorally) depict the presumed modification of the cluster concept we might face in the light of I4.0. It should be noted that '*stretching*' bears resemblance to the term of 'global cluster network', coined by Bathelt and Li (2014), which covers the system of ties and relations among firms located in clusters. It refers to both trans-local linkages between industrial clusters, but also local linkages within the same cluster. As argued by Turkina, Van Assche and Kali (2016), the recognition in the literature that the network of both local and trans-local (external) linkages are essential for a cluster firm's access to knowledge, encouraged scholars to go beyond the simple local-global dichotomy and adopt a network view of industrial clusters.

Internationalisation can be a channel facilitating more cluster heterogeneity, allowing the incorporation of the unrelated knowledge, preventing a lock-in situation and helping to sustain innovativeness and growth (Dohse, Fornahl & Vehrke, 2018). The need of heterogenous external knowledge can be derived from the cluster-life-cycle (CLC) model (Brenner & Schlump, 2011; Fornahl, Hassink & Menzel, 2015; Menzel & Fornahl, 2010). It assumes that the cluster goes through different developmental stages (emergence, growth, sustainment and decline). As argued by Buciuni and Pisano (2015), clusters can decline for two primary reasons. First, because other competing clusters can gain an advantage (out-perform these clusters) or second, because agglomeration economies would dissipate, due to changes in technology, competitive dynamics or some other reason. Similarly, as shown by Turkina and Van Assche (2018), the cluster's technological base is far more than previously subject to the resident firms' capabilities of sourcing the distant knowledge. When talking about *stretching*, it should be mentioned that Chapman, MacKinnon and Cumbers (2004) distinguish between geographical diversification and sectoral diversification as forms of cluster renewal (adaptability leading to change and continuity, simultaneously). It thus can be considered as stimulated by the influx of novelty from other sectors within a region or through extra-regional linkages (Njøs & Jakobsen, 2016).

The processes of *hubbing* and *blending* could also be seen in the context of inter-clustering—still a nascent research field (Lorenzen & Mudambi, 2013; Goerzen, 2018). Inter-clustering might be regarded as a specific form of increasing the geographical scope and/or sectoral scope. Franco and Esteves (2020) see inter-clustering centred around knowledge sharing and learning as specific inter-organisational relations, which contributes to regional competitiveness (Dohse, 2007; Schüßler, Decker & Lerch, 2013). Inter-clustering is also perceived as a synonym for co-operation (Cusin & Loubaresse, 2018), providing benefits for participating clusters (Schüßler, Decker & Lerch, 2013).

Stretching processes might be also seen as the accessing and sourcing of different knowledge bases (synthetic, analytical or symbolic) from different geographical scales (from regional to global). It can happen thanks to different mechanisms—market forces, networks (e.g. alliances), spill-overs (e.g. mobility) and hierarchies (e.g. FDI) (Bellandi, Chaminade & Plechero, 2018).

The processes of *blending* and *hubbing* described below also mirror some calls (Park, 2018) that innovative cluster policies must respond to new industrial challenges through facilitating cross-sectoral value chains and strengthening internationalisation. *Stretching* (*hubbing*, but also to some extent *blending*, providing it involves an external dimension) might be seen as a strategic coupling of regional and extra-regional assets, which enables the path creation and emergence of new economic activities (MacKinnon, Dawley, Pike & Cumbers, 2019; Chandrashekar & Subrahmanya, 2019).

Blending strategy aims at the upgrading of the cluster and buttressing the innovation capabilities of incumbent firms through facilitating the mixing of different but somehow related competencies (Gancarczyk & Bohatkiewicz, 2018). This strategy implies expanding the industrial scope of the cluster by stimulating the collaboration between firms in related branches and those with different but similar knowledge. It stresses the regional dimension and can be associated with RV (Boschma & Frenken, 2011; Cooke, 1992; Cooke, Uranga & Etxebarria, 1997; Uyarra, 2010).

Blending means the co-operation between related entities within a region (Njøs & Jakobsen, 2016; Njøs et al., 2017a). It is not only linked to the concept of RV (Frenken, Van Oort & Verburg, 2007), but also regional branching (Boschma & Frenken, 2011; Boschma & Giannelle, 2014), and stresses different dimensions of proximity, such as cognitive and organisational, rather than purely industrial specialisation and (only) geographical vicinity. The region is in the centre of this strategy. *Blending* strategy stimulates knowledge spill-overs between related sectors and their players, i.e. it encourages the cross-industry innovation (Enkel & Gassmann, 2010) and facilitates 'mixing' of different but associated competences. *Blending* should lead to the expansion of the cluster's industrial scope by promoting co-operation, knowledge exchange and learning between companies representing related branches. This strategy, however, runs the risk of stimulating 'unproductive' networking (too many differences). *Blending* is meant as a counter-balance to traditional sector specialisation (Cooke, 2012) as it backs a more diverse system. In consequence, it modifies the definition of cluster, stipulating that this is an agglomeration of units belonging to related industries.

Hubbing strategy means that a cluster creates new connections or assemblage points outside the original cluster core area, and as such, is linked to the exploitation of geographic scale. This process enables the development of specialised clusters by building extra-regional pipelines and establishing relations with specialised external actors. *Hubbing* can be associated with the concept of global pipelines, regarded commonly as drivers of innovation (Bathelt,

Malmberg & Maskell, 2004) and learning, thanks to their role of connecting the highly competent actors of innovation systems (Malerba, 2002). *Hubbing* denotes the geographical expansion of cluster linkages, i.e. the increase of the geographic areas of impact (Njøs & Jakobsen, 2016). *Hubbing* strategy underscores the building of external linkages, based on a cluster's sector-specific expertise and utilisation of scale economies. *Hubbing* brings the risk that fostering extra-regional specialised ties happens at the expense of building linkages among local firms in related branches. *Hubbing*, nevertheless, allows the cluster to establish 'satellites' or 'nodes' in external, highly relevant national or even international milieux. These extra-regional networks may stimulate the innovativeness, learning and development, but may pose a challenge to encourage and maintain a local buzz.

In this place, the relations between internationalisation of the cluster and the *stretching* processes, in particular, the *hubbing* should be accurately defined (Götz, 2020). Internationalisation, as presented commonly in existing literature, encompasses mostly, the processes of foreign expansion by local constituting firms, either in the form of the export or a more advanced mode of an international venture, including FDI, or by attracting new investors from abroad. CO may obviously, and usually does, play an essential role in facilitating these relations. *Hubbing* is understood as a geographical expansion of the cluster, as gaining new members and new territory. Here, the 'reaching out' is more the search for sustained/increased competitiveness, rather than the result of revealed competitiveness. This activity, though, might be considered as a particular type/mode of cluster internationalisation along export or FDI lines. It is clear that the relationship between pure internationalisation and *hubbing* is complicated and requires some de-limitation (Figure 4.6).

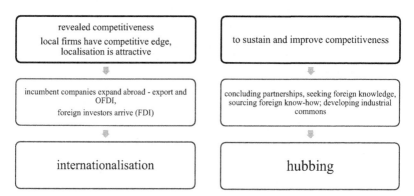

Figure 4.6 Internationalisation vs. *hubbing*

Source: Author's own proposal

In many studies so far, the external cluster linkages seem to have been understood in terms of internationalisation (Njøs et al., 2017a, b). The importance of extra-regional ties for cluster evolution requires taking into account nuances, such as context, as well as the diversified role of MNEs and their relations. By investigating one of Norway's strongest industry clusters, the sub-sea cluster in Hordaland county, Njøs et al. (2017a) demonstrate that MNEs-out (cluster inhabiting firms which venture abroad) bring about more specialisation to cluster renewal, by contrast, MNEs-in (incoming foreign enterprises) contribute to diversification. In light of the above, it is justified to argue that 'MNEs-in' and 'MNEs-out' satisfy the basic definition of cluster internationalisation (Jankowska & Götz, 2018). Yet, it contributes to the cluster adaptability and renewal, i.e. simultaneous processes of continuation (extension of practices) and change (novelty), by ensuring some balance between specialisation and diversification (Njøs et al., 2017a) (Figure 4.7). It can, however, also be provided, thanks to the *stretching—hubbing*, and most probably, *blending* (both *related and unrelated variety*).

Grillitsch et al. (2018) argue that positive regional/structural change, which can happen through the industrial development path, is subject to the 'opportunity space'. This 'opportunity space', i.e. the room for manoeuvre for makeover of the region, depends on whether the region is characterised by the specialisation (interactions traded and non-traded in a given field, including learning and innovation), the RV (potential of diversification drawing on similar knowledge) or *the unrelated variety* (combination of

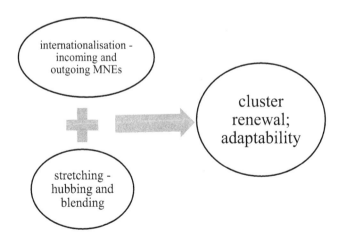

Figure 4.7 Internationalisation and *hubbing* of the cluster

Source: Author's own proposal

analytical, synthetic and symbolic knowledge), and whether the potential change is confined to the concrete geographic location, or it can happen in an abstract economic space (which allows for some external linkages). According to Grillitsch et al. (2018), it is, in fact, this under-appreciated concept of *unrelated variety* (typical for metropolitan areas), which seems to offer most possibilities for the industrial development path. Findings of research on the ongoing digital business transformation allow us to claim that this fourth industrial revolution might constitute a particular evolution from 'specialisation and concrete localisation' towards '*unrelated variety* and the growing importance of abstract space'. In other words, I4.0 could imply the transition of clusters (understood as specialised geographically and concentrated) towards diversified and more spatially abstract concepts; thus, supporting the hypothesis of more diversified and less focused clusters in the era of I4.0.

Digital technologies and infrastructure can enhance, extend and enrich interactions among economic agents (Autio & Thomas, 2016), thereby influencing the *stretching* processes. The digital disruption materialises via 'digital affordances'—defined as *possibilities* to perform existing functions more effectively or to perform entirely new functions (Autio, Nambisan, Thomas & Wright, 2018; Autio, 2017). These affordances can drive the business model innovation (BMI) and emergence of a distinctive type of cluster—entrepreneurial ecosystem (see also Feldman, Siegel & Wright, 2019). Whereas classic clusters focus on spatial affordances, entrepreneurial ecosystems are built upon digital affordances. It means that an entrepreneurial ecosystem constitutes such a cluster type, which is not specific to a particular sector or technology (Autio, Nambisan, Thomas & Wright, 2018). Entrepreneurial ecosystems, in contrast to classic clusters, put the emphasis on the exploitation of so-called digital affordances. They are organised around the discovery and pursuit of entrepreneurial opportunity and concentrate on BMI. Entrepreneurial ecosystems foster voluntary horizontal knowledge spill-overs and searching for cluster-external entrepreneurial opportunities. Although, not all, many features of entrepreneurial ecosystems seem to resemble the combination of RV and IC explored in this volume.

The issues incorporated in this volume seem to relate to the four aspects identified by Hassink, Isaksen and Trippl (2019), as critical for regional industrial path development. ICs might be linked to the (1) 'expectations', and to (2) 'how non-firm actors such as users, universities, intermediaries and policy actors shape the regional development'. The problem of (3) 'inter-path relations and interdependencies between multiple established paths, established paths and new paths, as well as multiple emerging paths' may all offer insight to the concept of RV and *blending* processes as

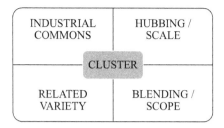

Figure 4.8 Key concepts which frame the analysis
Source: Author's own proposal

discussed in this volume. *Hubbing, meanwhile,* might be seen as reflecting the need for more attention to be paid to the (4) 'multi-scalarity of sources, relations and influences'.

Summing up, the framework for discussion is built around the concepts of (Figure 4.8):

- the RV, associated with such terms as 'smart or diversified specialisation' (McCann & Ortega-Argilés, 2014; Foray, David & Hall, 2009; Foray, 2014) or 'territorial servitisation', which implies local execution of various GVC activities, rather than single specialised slices.
- the ICs, which are understood as locally bound resources, agglomeration externalities, which draw on the triple helix concept (Leydesdorff, 2012; Etzkowitz, 2012).

If ICs are viewed as local externalities, scale economies or middle-ground activities; then RV, understood in terms of dynamic, complementary externalities, including the knowledge flows, might be seen as part of IC; or even as a specific section of IC.

Part III

Cluster as Provider of Industrial Commons and Related Variety Undergoing the Stretching Process

5   HAv Hamburg Aviation Cluster

Regional Specialisation and Cluster Profile

Aerospace is a highly clustered industry with firms displaying significant differences along different dimensions—geographical, internal capabilities or innovation outcomes (Speldekamp, Knoben & Saka-Helmhout, 2019). The aviation industry is one of the most complex and knowledge-intense industries (Redlich, Moritz & Wulfsberg, 2019), with a low degree of openness. Start-ups here are seldom able to access the respective large firms' infrastructure.

Hamburg aviation cluster represents one of the aerospace clusters identified in developed countries (Turkina & Van Assche, 2018). HAv is unique, as it combines both cluster and the Hamburg Metropolitan Region, which counts for more than 5.3 million residents (in Hamburg alone, 1.8 million), with a GDP of more than 205 billion euro. It encompasses four federal states and 20 counties with core industries such as aviation, renewable energy, logistics, maritime, life science, media and tourism.

The information concerning Hamburg's (regional/sectoral) specialisation (RV) can be found on the S3 Platform—Research and Innovation Strategy for Smart Specialisation—which is a free online tool and a comprehensive guide for creating, monitoring and updating Smart Specialisation Strategies (http://relatedvariety.s3platform.eu/results.php?region=Hamburg, accessed 15.01.2019). The RV analysis, available on the online S3 Platform, shows first, a particular region, and the sectors it is hosting; next, it filters these sectors that fulfil the criteria of location quotient (LQ) (sector specialisation in regional employment), i.e. are concentrated with critical mass. It also offers insight into those sectors, which have patent specialisation and are correlated. In Hamburg apparently, it is known as the 'manufacture of other transport equipment'.

In Germany, the major spatial agglomerations of the aviation industry can be found in the Metropolitan Region of Hamburg which specialises in civil aviation, and in Bavaria, where several sites of the Airbus Military and Defence segment are located (Buxbaum-Conradi, 2018). The aerospace LQ, which informs what makes a region 'unique' in comparison to the national average, equals 4.4 for Hamburg, implying that this sector is more than four times more concentrated in the region than the national average (55th HAv Forum, June, 2019). More than 41 thousand people have been employed in the aerospace sector, indicating the workforce's growth of 3% in the period, 2012–2017. The per capita value added of 126,000 euros, generated by 41,200 employees, in around 300 companies of the aviation sector in the Hamburg Metropolitan Region, exceeds the economic performance of the whole metropolitan region (74,599 euros per capita), as revealed by the market analysis, jointly produced by the VDI/VDE Institute for Innovation and Technology and Hamburg Aviation (Die Luftfahrt-Branche in der Metropolregion Hamburg, 2019). It implies the industry's higher than average productivity. The activities of HAv cover the related sectors of aeronautics (mathematics, engineering and lighter flight objects), aviation (engineering, design and manufacturing of aircraft) and aerospace (satellites, missiles and aircraft spaceships).

Aviation has a long tradition in Hamburg; hence, the cluster development reflects the path dependence processes from the early pioneers at the start of the 20th century (Buxbaum-Conradi, 2018). Aircraft were being built and tested in Hamburg, already in 1909. The foundation stone of the airport was laid in 1911. In the 1920s and 1930s, aircraft manufacture in Hamburg blossomed, but the military appropriated it during WW2. Aircraft, once again, were being produced in Hamburg in the mid-1950s, and Lufthansa built its technical base in 1955. In 1969, the Franco-German Airbus programme—critical as it turned out for the whole region—was initiated.

HAv is considered as the world's third most significant cluster of the aerospace industry after Seattle, with Boeing Headquarters and Toulouse hosting the Airbus Headquarters (Buxbaum-Conradi, 2018).

Cluster Structure and Activities

Hamburg Aviation is a cluster, in terms of spatial agglomeration of related sectors, but also, in terms of CO. Today's cluster HAv e.V. understood as registered association with the proper cluster management, was born in 2011, but the Hamburg Aviation Initiative was set up, previously, in 2001. The mission of HAv is to build aircraft, in particular cabins, to optimise the operation of air transport systems, to provide various aviation-related services and to master specialisation in aviation IT and communications.

HAv regards itself as a powerful alliance gathering business, science and politics, which launches various aviation-related initiatives and projects. Whereas the Aviation Network embraces all members; the HAv office is responsible for running the projects. The HAv's ultimate goals consist in the networking of firms and other institutions, promoting the growth of specialist personnel, expanding the transfer of knowledge and improving the local business environment. It also seeks to diagnose, and subsequently, fill the possible gaps in the process chain, to generate more innovations and extend areas of competency. The HAv activities encompass various formats. There are tailor-made events with intensive networking—the largest being the Hamburg Aviation Forum, which takes place three times a year. Here, an average of 200 participants come together and exchange views on trends and technologies in aviation. Other topics that are dealt with in Bar Camps or workshops, for example, range from employer branding and financing to new forms of co-operation. Crystal Cabin Awards awarded by an international jury in various categories can be imagined to be a bit like the aviation industry's 'Oscars'.

Three major players of HAv are Airbus, Lufthansa Technik and Hamburg Airport. Airbus factory is the place where the entire A320 family of aircraft is constructed, and where the section assembly, interior fitting and painting of the A380 (end of production from 2021, announced in February, 2019) take place, as well as essential processes in the construction of the new, long-haul A350. Lufthansa Technik AG headquartered in Hamburg is the world's leading provider of aircraft maintenance, repair and overhaul (MRO) services. Hamburg Airport is, not only the oldest airport in the world, still based at its original location; but also, is one of the world's most modern airports, with more than 14 million passengers every year.

Around this big trio, more than 300 SMEs, of suppliers and service providers, have gathered with a total of more than 40,000 highly qualified personnel. The HAv cluster members (www.hamburg-aviation.de/mitglied.html) comprise large manufacturing companies, as well as small consulting firms. All are obviously active in the metropolitan region, although, often headquartered in other cities. They can be HAv members, as long as they are connected to HAv's critical supply chain. This business ecosystem is complemented with teaching, training, research institutions, excellent universities and leading research labs. Prominent players are the associations, institutes and research facilities, plus Hamburg's four universities. The Hamburg Business Development Corporation (HWF) and the Ministry of Economy, Transport and Innovation (BWVI) have also been members from the very beginning. Besides, there are numerous sponsoring members (Buxbaum-Conradi, 2018).

These entities and their activities cover the whole value chain of aviation and complete the life cycle of an aircraft: from the development, manufacturing and assemblage, to the air transportation system, MRO, to final recycling. It sees itself as the international centre of expertise for 'new flying'.

Core competences comprise aircraft, transport and cabin systems. Although HAv covers every facet of aviation, it has a particular strength and competitive advantage in interior fittings and the design of aircraft cabins. According to official data from the European Cluster Collaboration Platform (www. clustercollaboration.eu), HAv's key industries include: Aerospace Vehicles and Defence, and Metalworking Technology. The Technology fields, which are covered, encompass Aeronautical Technology/Avionics and Aircraft.

In 2008, HAv won the Leading-Edge Cluster competition organised by the Federal Ministry of Education and Research and is benefitting beside the 'Signalling-Effect' from wide-ranging research support (Cantner, Graf & Töpfer, 2015; Audretsch, Lehmann & Menter, 2016; Rothgang et al., 2017). In 2014, it received the GOLD Label for Cluster Management Excellence by the European Commission, thereby ranking as one of the Top 40 clusters in Europe. It is also one of the winners of the 'Ausgezeichnete Orte im Land der Ideen' 2016 competition and benefits from public funds of the senate in Hamburg (Buxbaum-Conradi, 2018).

In 2014, Hamburg was selected by the EU Commission as one of six model regions for modern cluster policy, aiming at growth innovation and competitiveness (www.hamburg.de/wirtschaft/clusterpolitik-modellregion/). The city, as represented by the Ministry, works at bridging its eight clusters, and making them work together. As expressed by one of the interviewed COs, (CO1) 'During the severe economic and financial crisis of 2008+ many feared the slowdown, a significant deterioration of performance by the local economy, yet it did not happen, luckily. It is impossible to define how much it resulted from the cluster policy and the mindset adopted in the region. Nevertheless, it is very likely that without such an approach, the crisis would have unfolded much worse'. Cluster orientation—free Hanseatic City of Hamburg cluster policy—is like DNA of the region, which may, in turn, make the region more resilient to external shocks.

As such, the metropolitan region of Hamburg is plugged into the global network of mainly civil aerospace manufacturing, via the anchor company, Airbus, which has, in fact, been organising and co-ordinating since the 1970s, the whole European Aerospace Industry, by connecting firms and regions in the global network of production relations (Buxbaum-Conradi, 2018). Airbus was meant to be a European counter-balance to the strong US aerospace industry around Boeing. Still, as countries involved in this project, favoured their own domestic companies' participation, a fragmented industry structure with a high number of 'supplying' SMEs emerged (Turkina, Van Assche & Kali, 2016; Buxbaum-Conradi, 2018). Although, not a complete success, the Airbus production network, indeed, incarnates the European economic integration. In fact, due to the peculiarities of this project, development, management and manufacturing of the different aircraft programmes are conducted in Germany, France, Great Britain and Spain. Core competencies of the German sites are in the domains of cabin, fuselage and tail units. Compared to Toulouse (Airbus HQ), the economic structure in Hamburg is dominated by very small and SMEs in business-related service industries (mainly engineering service providers).

Summing up, business, academia, associations and local authorities form the HAv cluster, which aims at advancing the region as an excellent aviation centre. They jointly pursue a goal of developing and networking the R&D areas and offering high-quality products and services for the aviation of the future. This makes the metropolitan region, the third-biggest site in the civil aviation industry worldwide.

6 Findings and Discussion

Provision of ICs in HAv

Basic Infrastructure

The HAv's strength can be attributed chiefly to the geographic concentration of firms, universities, labs and research institutions, to their close networking with major players, i.e. Airbus, Lufthansa Technik and the Hamburg airport; and their competencies in specific areas along the entire value chain. Special attention is drawn to sustainable activities, aimed at attracting the next generation of educated staff and developing highly competent aviation personnel. It is provided by HCAT+, which offers a unique infrastructure for connecting teaching, practice and research activities, which are pre-dominantly managed by ZAL—responsible for application-oriented research. The strategy adopted in 2014, foresees 'A New Kind of Aviation'. It aims at making flying in the future more economical, more ecological, more comfortable, more flexible, more reliable and more connected. To fulfil these ambitious goals, HAv members work closely together on the construction of aircraft and cabins, and their respective systems, on optimisation of aviation services; on improving the efficiency of the air transportation system, as well as on further development of aviation-related IT and communication systems. HAv has also benefited from external funding and participated in numerous research and development projects.

Critical for the HAv's pool of local commons are these institutions:

- Hanse Aerospace e.V. can be regarded as SME's voice in the region (www.hanse-aerospace.net/). Founded in 1996, it represents the interests of companies and suppliers of the aerospace industry and is perceived as a counter-balance to mighty regional player, Airbus. It provides members with specialised advice and co-ordinates communication and relations with local government bodies, to address specific infrastructural issues.

- HECAS—Hanseatic Engineering & Consulting Association e.V. is an association comprising engineering and business consultant service providers located in the region, who are active in the aerospace sector (www.hecas-ev.de). HECAS considers itself, as the interface between the aerospace industry and local government, working towards keeping jobs in the region. The competencies of its members encompass the following: aerodynamics, consulting, construction and development, computing and testing, software engineering and technical documentation. HECAS is also a member of HAv, HCAT and ZAL, which indicates the deep inter-weaving of local economic, political and scientific actors in the region.
- BDLI (Bundesverband der Deutschen Luft- und Raumfahrtindustrie), the German Aerospace Industries Association, with more than 230 companies, is the primary industry representative for the aerospace sector in the whole of Germany. As the voice of German aerospace, BDLI participates actively in dialogue with political institutions, regional authorities, trade associations and the chamber of commerce, as well as governments at home and abroad (www.bdli.de/en).
- DLR (Deutsches Zentrum für Luft- und Raumfahrt), the German Aerospace Centre, acts as the national aeronautics and space research centre. Serving as Germany's space agency, DLR has been given responsibility for the planning and implementation of the German space programme (www.dlr.de/dlr/en/).
- HCAT, the Hamburg Centre for Aviation Training, works to safeguard the highly qualified workforce and human capital for the aerospace industry in the region (www.hcatplus.de; Buxbaum-Conradi, 2018). It sees itself as a co-ordinator and moderator, in terms of training and qualifying personnel, developing new approaches to cultivating talents and providing vocational and academic education.
- ZAL (Zentrum for Angewandte Luftfahrtforschung GmbH) Hamburg's Centre of Applied Aeronautical Research, founded in 2016, is the technological R&D network of the civil aviation industry in the Hamburg Metropolitan Region (www.zal.aero/home/). It is an interface between academic, research institutions, the aviation sector and the City of Hamburg, and one of the most advanced German technological research centres with impressive facilities. ZAL's focus is on the integration and industrialisation of aviation technologies. Projects developed here are jointly owned and produced by all participants, working together as partners. Technology fields are organised in the three so-called Centres of Competence (CoC)—Aircraft Manufacturing & MRO, Cabin & Systems and Digitalisation Technologies. These centres cover various aspects of I4.0, such as new business models, additive manufacturing

or predictive maintenance. ZAL runs in the formula of a public-private partnership (PPP), linking giants such as Airbus and Lufthansa Technik, with many small start-ups. ZAL acts, not only as a provider of ICs, thanks to its Tech Centre, yet it also stimulates the development of RV, due to dedicated, diversified CoCs. ZAL, and likewise Airbus, may also be regarded as cluster technology gatekeepers/anchor tenants, i.e. the key actors playing a central position with the capability of pulling around other members (Hervas-Oliver & Albors-Garrigos, 2014; Morrison, 2008; Baglieri, Cinici & Mangematin, 2012).

Besides these dedicated bodies, the Metropolitan Hamburg Region can boast having four universities, which are committed to teaching and research, in the field of aviation. These include the following: Hamburg University of Applied Sciences (HAW Hamburg); Helmut Schmidt University of the Federal Armed Forces, Hamburg; Hamburg University of Technology (TUHH) and the University of Hamburg. Local authorities, who play a crucial role in founding many initiatives, are also involved.

Thanks to the various projects conducted, the cluster can expand its core competencies. Conducted initiatives range from research on fuel cells as a possible source of energy; acoustic improvements in the cabin, maintenance methods for new materials, to the optimisation of airport processes. Specific novel initiatives are born in the most significant players, such as Airbus. In 2018, Airbus launched the I4.0 think-tank and lab learning, and set up 'Factory of the Future' to ease the digital transformation for its staff (work clothes: gloves, glasses, exoskeleton and smart t-shirt). Despite these multiple activities and, the fact, that Airbus interacts with different firms, its role as a dominant integrator of HAv knowledge is assessed as relatively weak (Buxbaum-Conradi, 2018), although, it indisputably impacts upon the whole cluster performance (Aznar-Sanchez & Carretero-Gómez, 2016; Lazerson & Lorenzoni, 2008; Buciuni & Pisano, 2015).

Three significant areas of work and pillars of HAv cluster are research and innovation moderated by the ZAL; skills and expertise moderated by the HCAT, and supply chain and SMEs moderated by the Hansa Aerospace and HECAS. HAv, and likewise seven other Hamburg clusters, work in the triple helix format, so it satisfies all necessary criteria of co-operation among academia, business and public authorities.

The Uniqueness of Aviation and Limited Implementation of I4.0

A total of 26 in-depth and semi-structured interviews, conducted in HAv in 2019, were anonymised and classified as interviews with CRs, CEs, CCs, COs or CSs, respectively. Actually, all interviewed HAv representatives, unanimously, and on many occasions, stressed the uniqueness of the aviation industry. It is understood in terms of high-entry barriers, a closed market of oligopolistic nature, political dimension reflected in Airbus being a European political integration project, and concerning I4.0, with less than might be expected, digital technologies' penetration. This relatively lower I4.0 susceptibility, as compared for instance, with the automotive sector, implies continuous importance of the job delivered by humans and limited possibilities to completely replace employees with robots. A particularly sober approach among CRs might reflect the fact that I4.0 is a fashionable trend, a policy and a discourse, advocating the digital transformation, but not yet, much adopted by all local firms.

The peculiarity of the aviation sector and the importance of a few large players globally are also reflected in the composition of HAv. In particular, it implies that Airbus strongly dominates the Hamburg cluster. In some experts' opinion, there is a discrepancy between how HAv (as a PPP) presents itself in public, and how successfully it performs. (CS2) 'Airbus is the largest player, creates jobs, has shares in ZAL, but is surrounded by suspicion. Industry 4.0 and related digital transformations are a trend promoted by the German government. However, most of the suppliers on the local scale, lack such knowledge and skills'.

The uniqueness of HAv rests in the fact that it is the third largest civil aviation place, after Toulouse and Seattle (altogether, they make up 80% of the global aeronautical industry). Hosting Airbus means a unique cluster setting, however, with dominance and asymmetry. Nevertheless, this results from the quasi-oligopolistic nature of the aviation market. Despite causing much power imbalances, Airbus, thanks to its geographically dispersed production chain, links various places with their local networks. Airbus is indeed the centre of gravity in the region, and the aviation industry is seen by some as a dominant player, abusing its privileged position, by others as a critical orchestrator and conductor of relations. (CE2) 'Whereas politicians involved with their agenda (representing different federal German states engaged in HAv) might cause tensions and work at the crossroads; it is Airbus, which binds that altogether'.

The focus in HAv is on later value chain stages, on manufacturing, production, assembly of cabin, wings, tails; i.e. not the most knowledge-intensive research, and development stages carried out in labs. Hence, in the opinion of some experts, HAv seems to be missing the truly knowledge-intensive stages, in terms of I.40.

HAv and related institutions like ZAL see their role in raising awareness among SMEs of the digital transformation and providing the extra push to move towards I4.0. Thanks to a neutral networking platform, ZAL seeks to provide exchange in all various directions and to link partners, assuring a level playing field (eye-to-eye). So, small firms should not fear losing their independence, vis-a-vis the large player. How it plays out, in reality, brings a mixed assessment.

In the eyes of HAv representatives, I4.0 seems to be a common thread of various initiatives undertaken. It is in the back of minds and activities of cluster members seen as an inevitable challenge and a chance at the same time. As such, only some of the I4.0 technologies are applied, like artificial intelligence (AI). However, against the digital revolution background, it should be stressed that aviation is a specific industry, and unlike the automotive one, much less digitised or autonomously integrated. Cobots, digital twins or exoskeletons are more common as automatisation and digitisation can only support or complement humans.

HAv regards the I4.0 as one of the strategic topics. However, the implementation track record among firms is mixed. (CC1) 'We are using some technologies of I4.0, but not all of them, so we adopt I4.0 to some extent only'. It is perceived that this implementation should come naturally, from the need of firms themselves. (CC1) 'You look for the technologies and chose what suits you'. (CC12) 'We are a small and rather young firm, we do not have many activities in terms of I4.0, but we are looking into it, to have more digital production'. (CC6) 'Industry 4.0 could be understood as morphing into a paperless company, having automated processes, but if you see it as fully digitalised product chains, then we are not a I4.0 company, but we are heading that way, implementing some solutions. We are on the road but have not yet arrived'. The other firms are more upbeat and can claim—(CC2) 'Yes, 100%, we are an I4.0 digital company in two ways. Internally, we work and use digital tools; we are all digital natives. From the external perspective, products that we provide, rely very much on artificial intelligence, and when it comes to creating the scenarios, it is also based on big data'. (CC10) 'Thanks to digital technologies, we can streamline everything, to collect, analyse, monitor, to control quality, operations, financial issues, sale . . . However, we cannot transform the way of working in some short period, it is very difficult; all the documentation is created, based on years, we try to improve digital solutions, but it will take time'. As put by one company (CC7), 'there is much hype about I4.0 and SME's want to make its USP (unique selling points), seize the opportunity, but they might be dangerous endeavours'.

Companies benefit from cluster membership, as it brings the possibility to exchange both the views and experience of other firms. It also helps to make progress, in terms of adopting I4.0. (CC11) 'Networking with other industry participants is crucial. It offers the possibility to exchange ideas, and the implementation of ideas with other industries'. (CC12) 'Cluster can help us implementing new technologies, if there are some case studies, so that we can learn from others, exchange information, know about available options'.

Some companies praise, not only the right connections, in terms of hearing from other suppliers, but closer relations via association to Airbus (the primary customer for most of them), but also good relationships with politicians, as well as the access to specialised knowledge, as the profile and curricula of local universities in Hamburg or Bremen are better aligned with these firms' 'aviation' portfolio. (CE4) 'Policy support makes a difference; this involvement helps, moderate these new mega-trends'.

In fact, in the opinion of many local actors, it is difficult to determine if HAv is a truly I4.0 cluster. (CO1) 'I would not call HAv—a I4.0 cluster, although it is affected by digital business transformation'. They admit that HAv office is trying a lot to accommodate these new possibilities of digitalisation and adapt them to the members' needs, for instance, by setting up the HAV connect platform (www.hav-connect.aero/). Likewise, regular 'old school' events, like HAv Forum, which offers the possibility of extensive networking, have facilitated some digital transformation, along with new formats like Bar Camps, devoted to innovations. Not only is HAv office engaged in the promotion of I4.0. Hansa Aerospace sees its task explicitly, as accompanying firms in their digital transformation (Hanse-Aerospace: Ihr Wegbereiter für Industrie 4.0). In some opinions, this distant digital communication (part of digital transformation) is a threat to clusters; a threat, which is unavoidable. That being said, clusters might try to harness it for their benefits—do something to make the communication within clusters easier, to smooth it, and be a digital interface between cluster members. (CE3) 'If it is going to be easier to work with any company on this planet, then the cluster needs to make the co-operation between cluster members within-the-cluster, even easier'.

Asymmetry, Legitimacy and Networking

The highlighted specificity of the aviation industry in general, as a market dominated by few, if not just two major players, is reflected in the HAv cluster, in particular. The presence of the major actor, i.e. Airbus company, confers strength and prestige for the HAv. Hosting such an actor is undoubtedly a reason to be proud for the cluster managers and local policymakers. Nevertheless, it is also a source of significant concern for many small cluster players. They admit benefits from the proximity of the main contractor, although, they point out huge asymmetry, in terms of power relations. Fortunately, to address this imbalance, HAv managers are seeking continuously to provide a level playing field for all its members. The possibility to talk 'eye-to-eye' with the giant, is one of the significant benefits of cluster membership—it empowers the small- and medium-sized actors. This legitimacy, deriving from the fact of being a HAv member, facilities the relations outside the cluster, as it sends a positive signal and increases the firms' visibility. Networking and vivid business relations alleviate the liability of smallness, suffered by most small firms. As it seems, cluster internalises for its members, the positive scale effects and agglomeration externalities. Thus, it may emulate the more favourable conditions enjoyed by large companies.

As stressed by almost all respondents, aviation is indeed a unique industry. It is like a natural monopoly or oligopoly market. (CE2) 'You simply have only two-three big players worldwide, so you are happy to have one of them in your cluster'. Nevertheless, as argued by some (CC3) 'Airbus is the largest player, but in the end, it is an assembly company, it needs input from other firms. HAv is not only Airbus, but there are also many small innovative companies round there'.

In the opinion of most cluster members, business networks are critical, and co-operation with complementary firms matters most. (CE2) 'Being here you let the other know that you exist, administrative umbrella, or even knowledge, comes second'. (CC9) 'From our view, the most important benefit of membership are the linkages to other companies, potential customers'.

Proximity is central, in the opinion of cluster firms, as it generates trust, which is critical for co-operation. Frequent face-to-face contacts reduce mistrust. (CC1) 'We are here within 20 minutes of a car drive, no language barriers, jointly shared values, same way of doing something; it helps, for instance, while conducting large EU projects'. Spatial closeness is essential for some firms, like those who deliver the engines, also due to classic transportation costs.

Business relations, networks and connections provided in HAv are critical. As stressed by one company—meeting people daily, talking, having lunch together, creates trust. (CC1) 'We are all humans, so knowing each other is critical for co-operation, and being part of the cluster enables this. This feeling of belonging matters in external relations. It is not easy for us to contact large companies; cluster helps us to establish contacts. The barrier of communicating is reduced; everybody knows each other. You always have the feeling that you are speaking to someone you already know'. Membership confers, hence, a certain legitimacy. SMEs do not have sufficient business contacts, nevertheless, thanks to the cluster, they can talk to large firms on a level playing field. (CC1) 'For us, it was clear that as a small company, we will never go down that path alone, and we are dependent on large firms to collaborate'. Large companies or universities have their tools, budgets and have developed a set of relations. HAv membership means for many medium-sized companies, a real influence on strategy, selection and development of strategic priorities. (CC1) 'If you participate, your interest is put at a higher level. You play a role in something bigger'.

As the case of HAv shows, this feeling of belonging, being part of something larger, experienced by many members, is vital and cannot be overestimated, particularly for SMEs. It opens the doors, gives identity and confers the legitimacy. CCs almost unanimously agree that they definitely benefit most from business networking. HAv is a door-opener and treats all its members equally. (CC2) 'It is also a platform to be in media, to be present, to reach out, increase the exposure'. Being a member increases small firms' visibility; they can show their company to the broader public outside and also get larger market context. In the opinion of HAv companies, institutional and organisational support also matters much, because of the uniqueness of the industry with high entry barriers.

Regarding the business relations, HAv members almost unanimously agree, they are essential, and HAv is doing a tremendous job to facilitate this. This networking also enhances the exchange of knowledge, particularly, if one considers knowledge not in a narrow sense, but broader as a tacit or sticky knowledge, which requires face-to-face contact and implies innovative collaboration.

Time Decompression

Time dimension permeates the discussion on ICs. These, as the HAv case shows, are shaped by previous decisions (modularisation and offshoring leading to the destruction of local ties and disappearing industrial fabric) and influenced by future outlook (need to provide skills for next generations and anticipate future competences). So, what stands out in the provision of the HAv pool of ICs are beside the classic economies of scope or scale typical for clusters, the economies of time. It is because of the strong focus on developing future competences for aviation specialists.

Past decisions weigh on clusters' presence, like the decline of regional suppliers, resulting from the modulation process, adopted by Airbus. Previous developments have led to some local destruction and disappearance of indigenous business. Nevertheless, as being aware of the time dimension, local actors make a continuous effort to address future challenges, specifically, in terms of skills and competences. Thus, the erosion of value chain and as seen by some experts, the faltering or even dying industrial fabric, requires more concerted actions to restore the ICs, among others by focusing on training, education, skills in the aviation sector. The advantages of time decompression (diseconomies of time compression) reflect the gradual nature of the expertise building.

Following the modularisation strategy of Airbus, many local suppliers have been cut off from the production network, which destroyed existing trust relations. Previous idiosyncratic specifications were replaced by some standardised modules. Instead of the former, usually captive linkages among networks' actors, the common knowledge infrastructure is created in a horizontal global system of standard-setting organisations. Locally, this, unfortunately, has led to the disruption of existing inter-personal trust relations and specific disembedding processes (Buxbaum-Conradi, 2018).

Cluster experts argue that there used to be a tendency to make production and development decentralised, however, modularisation, not only proved to be hard, but it has also much affected the local cluster relationships. Now there seems to be a trend to reverse the previous strategy and to re-integrate production, vertically. (CS2) 'They have problems. The whole supply chain has been dying. Firms have to merge to survive; so, it seems they focus now more on training, education, consulting. Disappearing local suppliers constitute a real challenge for the local economy; this fabric needs to be re-instated'. Companies' representatives also stressed that due to austerity policies or costs optimisation, firms re-organised their qualification systems and the shortages now faced are the acute consequence of past decisions.

As argued by some firm's representative, for aeronautics, it is essential to remain specialised. Due to the competition and the role of experience, it seems inevitable, to develop the know-how, consequently and incrementally. It takes time to build expertise, to learn from mistakes, to know the problems, and know the consequences of them. (CC10) 'It takes years to reach high quality'.

Future Skills and Competences

Future skills and competencies (of not only white-collar aviation sector's specialists, but also blue-collar workers) feature high on the agenda of cluster actors. The need to predict and adequately address the challenges of future labour market necessitates the introduction of proper measures. Besides official entities tasked with such an issue (HCAT+), the cluster locally and endogenously, created a labour market with frequent job-hopping, as well as dedicated projects and programmes, all contributing to the development of future skills.

Firms' representatives stress that there is a growing need to produce more aircraft, mainly, as the market is dominated, in fact, by two large players. Unfortunately, there seems to be a shortage of skilled workers. There is not enough supply of trained technicians, particularly qualified blue-collar staff (not white-collar engineers). Therefore, qualifications are critical for the industry, for the region and the cluster. (CC4) 'If you are a company like Airbus, you have to react, to do something, to provide dual training like the apprenticeship. Nevertheless, to train a system engineer/mechanical engineer properly, you need at least three years. There are attempts to make up for this by offering some courses, but you cannot replace three years' education with a narrowly defined course. Although, it can be the only feasible solution for the moment'. Besides, young people seem not interested in this type of work, as training usually implies a reduction in salary and the job offered is rarely permanent, as there are generally fixed-time contracts. It makes the jobs unattractive, as they cannot guarantee a safe and stable future for young people.

Predicting and shaping future competences and skills takes place in different dimensions. Firstly, cluster management provides multiple possibilities. There are various events, training, presentations or courses, which centre upon the improvement of soft skills, digital competences, also related to I4.0. Secondly, a vital element, in fact, available thanks to the cluster's major attribute—co-location and proximity—is job switching. Skills not only develop via specific training or education, but also via moving from one job to another, by changing employers. It is obviously much easier within the cluster. Close localisation enables workers to change jobs between companies (job-hopping), and in fact, can strengthen the local labour market. The skills and competences acquired in that way are indeed, regarded as valuable. (CO1) 'The brain drain is there, but it is something in a net positive. Some companies lose workforce, the others gain, but it enables more adaptability to adverse shocks, and allows the region to grow'. Thirdly, there is a dedicated body the HCAT+, which is tasked with the development of new competencies, particularly in the aviation sector. Fourthly, and in relation to the latter, there are dedicated projects, which address this problem like DigiNet.Air run (2017–2021) by HCAT+ (www.diginetair.de). DigiNet.Air brings together SMEs (responsible for developing new concepts, in terms of future work 4.0); education (schools and universities tasked with developing future-oriented and demand-driven modules of teaching new skills and competences); and technology (labs and universities, in charge of developing and testing new solutions in the I4.0 area, demonstration, prototypes). DigiNet.Air, as a unique alliance, aims at countering the negative consequences of qualified labour skills' shortages, but also to adjust the teaching and training systems to modern challenges induced by the fourth industrial revolution. It, in turn, should help local SMEs to weather the potential labour market problems and boost the competitiveness of the aviation sector in the region. HCAT+ works on various aspects of qualification in the digital era and seeks to cater to the aviation and local market needs, by flexibly and jointly figuring out solutions, and by detecting and occupying the blind spots in the German education of aviation, not covered so far by schools or firms.

Cluster members prefer to talk about the 'brain circulation'—brain gains rather than brain loses, such as job switching might cause. Consequently, they confirm the earlier findings (Smith & Waters, 2005), which stipulate the importance of the movement of the highly skilled between local employers and the positive contribution of such rotations to the intra-regional transmission of expertise, knowledge spill-overs and the development of linkages among companies (Keeble, Lawson, Smith, Moore & Wilkinson, 1998; Storper & Scott, 1990). A high rate of intra-cluster mobility of the educated workforce, although it can bring non-trivial costs to employees or companies' managers (Fallick, Fleischman & Rebitzer, 2006), is usually associated with shorter unemployment periods and builds endogenously, a local, specialised labour market. It often also results in collective learning processes fostering creativity and entrepreneurship. Agglomeration or more accurately, cluster improves the co-ordination of labour market, accelerates the rate of interactions and facilitates the formation of human capital (Freedman, 2008).

Multiple projects backed by industry, the city and universities serve the purpose of developing skills for the next generation of aviation specialists. The Faszination Technik Klub has been set up. Lectures and events related to aviation, even for children and teenagers, are organised. DLR School Lab at the Hamburg University of Technology carries out technical and scientific experiments. It might mirror the fact that the necessary cluster evolution, as derived from the CLC approach, is already imprinted in HAv's activities (Tödtling, Sinozic & Auer, 2016). While HCAT+ is committed to future generation skills, the main task of another powerful actor in the region, ZAL, is to integrate these competencies within the region and its firms. The importance of 'people' and 'talents', as one of the significant trends, including action areas such as lifelong learning, attracting talents, developing new curricula or training for today's and future needs, can be found in a new strategy (55th HAv Forum, 2019). It reflects the ongoing, often disruptive processes taking place in the aviation industry, transforming it into a more broadly understood mobility concept, which, characterised by consolidation, shorter life cycles and fast ageing, require agile approaches.

Cultivating Commons

Providing ICs demands from HAv managers, but also all cluster stockholders, the efforts to literally take the common outside the bracket, as a shared element. That what divides, should be taken out of the cluster formula and focus should be on that what binds; 'commons' should be cultivated.

Various practices aim at improved smooth communication among members, orchestration of dispersed activities and integration of different, potentially interested actors.

The previous study dedicated to HAv revealed the importance of communication and identity building as pre-requisites for members' engagement (Hintze, 2018). In order to make CCs more involved in cluster activities (regional co-operation), it is critical to convince them about the need for identification with the cluster as such. It implies developing the cluster identity and creation of cluster brand, which members share, feel they belong to, and of which, they can be proud. It requires, in turn, appropriate communication, which happens at 'four floors' (Hintze, 2018; Putnam & Nicotera, 2009). It namely involves the internal interactions, external negotiating, cluster structures and rules/norms/standards, i.e. some code of conduct, which common language is, and the practice of doing things, a routine, e.g. for organising workshops. Only then, the proper all four floors communication can create the organisation, i.e. the cluster. This element of communication, and in result, the identity, also seems central for provision of IC, understood as a bundle of idiosyncratic assets, as a sort of public good. Brand/identity is like a quality label, something recognisable. It creates the image with which cluster members can easily associate (Morgulis-Yakushev & Sölvell, 2017).

Developing identity is a process, which takes time, needs routines and establishes some culture of co-operation, as uncertainty breaks only over the years. In the beginning, as stressed by cluster experts, any negotiations and talks took place, providing the non-disclosure agreement (NDA) had been signed. The mistrust was high. People were afraid of involuntary knowledge spill-overs. They needed comfortable conditions to co-operate; hence, the growing popularity of co-working spaces in Hamburg aimed at facilitating the exchange of knowledge and collaboration. The search for commons is visible, literally in actions aiming at better cross-clustering collaboration. There is a need to take the common, the shared issue 'outside the brackets', as some sort of binding. ZAL is thus, working more on developing a conducive environment for co-working, providing not just the space, but facilitating more interactions among their tenants, so that it could act as an integrator.

HAv-connect.aero, a platform managed by HAv, sets out to stimulate the information exchange. It can be accessed only by members and serves as an online forum, where interested parties can share their initiatives, apply jointly for projects or exchange documents. This platform is a real integrative tool, which may support the implementation of some digital technologies, as it allows for preparing, testing and developing solutions. Various groups are dealing with specific topics, integrating a different set of members, who encourage the exchange of information, work on some joint documents, preparation of meetings, sharing proposals or presentations after the sessions.

Co-opetition distinguishes clusters as economic categories; as a result, the need is to find possibilities to foster co-operation among competitors. Competition is a natural consequence of cluster, but the challenge for CO is to reduce the rivalry and cultivate the commons, to find the value-added that the co-operation could bring to all. Cluster co-opetition means that, sometimes, in some areas the entities co-operate, while at other times, they compete. (CO1) 'It is the task for cluster managers to take this competition outside the formula, and to find a common element which binds, which can be taken out of the bracket, as something all members share, can adhere to'. It is hence, necessary to identify and create possibilities for people to get together, to build up a relationship, so that there is a community. (CS1) 'They say in Hamburg—If you co-operate, you do not need a contract, you just need a handshake'.

Dark Sides

Regardless of the integrationist efforts by HAv managers and numerous natural benefits, the dark sides of cluster membership must not be ignored. Local firms and experts admit some tendencies of free riding, laziness among members, lack of interest in joint activities, unwillingness to participate in specific projects, as well as high, although, systematically falling, mistrusts and suspicion. Also, individual, well-meant, administrative decisions have caused more rivalry or damaged local relations, although, they were guided by good intentions. Besides, some competence shortages of often under-equipped members have already been mentioned. Experts highlight that trust issues in the local network, sometimes, impede collective action and joint R&D projects.

Cluster representatives regret that mutual relationships between HAv members and the HAv office seem a bit of a 'one-way' street. HAv, as the cluster office or umbrella organisation, co-ordinates various processes, provides matchmaking or facilitates collaboration. Members appreciate these efforts and see the value for money—and are ready to pay the membership fee, but they often do not provide feedback, are not interested in any follow-up or stay reluctant to get more engaged.

It is challenging to gather members together, not just because they have different interests, size or potential, but rather due to their unwillingness or some lack of conviction, that it makes sense. (CC5) 'HAv is doing much to support members. When a new project is being initiated, all are on board when it ends; it is just with a fraction of members, 30–40%. People are unwilling, lazy perhaps'. Success, also in digital transformation, requires joining forces across the board of all members.

However, as pointed out by some expert, innovations and co-operation in the HAv are tough, because of politicians' involvement (representatives of different federal states) and the natural need to pursue the demands of their respective local constituencies. There are tensions in this co-operation. (CE2) 'In such a constellation, you cannot easily bring innovation'.

ZAL—one of the major players—despite its merit, seems to be perceived by many local players with much scepticism. ZAL presents itself as an impartial partner that provides a platform where actors can meet 'eye-to-eye', on a level playing field. However, according to the study by Buxbaum-Conradi (2018), it is not commonly perceived as being 'neutral'. The power asymmetries among partners are visible in the working groups and technical domains. It deters smaller players, as they fear sharing expertise, and ideas are 'absorbed' afterwards, by the more powerful actors of the network. Universities' representatives also tend to complain that with the establishment of the ZAL, their specialised institutes now have to compete with additional actors for qualified personnel and funding.

Apparently, as seen by some cluster experts, the policy involvement might be even seen as unfavourable, as it can create more of the bad than the good, and therefore, generate more problems. Particular decisions become a liability for research institutions, not only in terms of increased bureaucracy and administrative burdens, but they produce more rivalry unintentionally, or cause the duplication of work. That 'created competition' might be the reason behind some negative assessments of the policymaker's involvement. As put by some expert (CS1): 'at the beginning all were competitors, the atmosphere was tough and thick, you could cut the air literally, and members promised—unless we sign the NDA (non-disclosure agreement), we will not talk, so mistrust was high; but now, after some years, they are more like friends'.

On a Final Note

Representing the world's third largest aviation hub, the HAv offers its members well-organised platforms, facilitating networking, thanks to the organisation of aviation forums, workshops and symposia. It enables collaborations with international clusters and facilitates missions to foreign markets. HAv, by its dedicated bodies, is also involved in assuring programmes for attracting the next generation of specialised personnel and helps to achieve better correspondence by teaching, practice and research in aviation engineering.

An essential resource of the HAv cluster is the knowledge infrastructure with laboratories, techno-centres and universities, which encourages researching the motto, 'a new kind of aviation'. Following the Järvi, Almpanopoulou and Ritala (2018) classification, it may be stated that HAv operates as knowledge ecosystems, searching within an identified knowledge domain, in opposition to the ecosystem, which is searching for a knowledge domain. In a knowledge ecosystem where a knowledge domain has already been identified, actors reveal problem- and solution-related knowledge, by participating in formal membership, gaining access to resources and their contributions are monitored (Järvi, Almpanopoulou & Ritala, 2018).

Geographical proximity facilitates daily, often informal interactions, which build trust and encourage collaboration, including sharing sensitive information and technology know-how (Dahl & Pedersen, 2004; Saxenian, 2000; Richardson, Yamin & Sinkovics, 2012). The findings of this research also confirm the time economies of clusters or time compression diseconomies, as it often takes years and decades to develop favourable social relations, stimulating networking (Anderson, Hakansson & Johanson, 1994; Dahl & Pedersen, 2004; Granovetter, 1985; Xu & McNaughton, 2006). HAv provides this fluidity of connections (Kuah, 2002) that certainly goes beyond the hierarchical network linkages.

To enrich the analysis and provide some triangulation, a short online questionnaire, which addresses studied issues, has been set. HAv representatives (officials and companies), as well as regional researchers involved in exploring clusters, were asked to address certain aspects. The results obtained (35 answers), although, in general, tend to confirm the presumed interdependencies, also revealed the avoidable in any community differences in opinions, including even strong emotional perceptions, and attitude ranging from very positive to harshly critical. It, however, confirms the unbiased composition of the sample.

The results of an anonymous online survey revealed that 77% agree (strongly agree and just agree) that the cluster facilitates digital transformation (I4.0), as it provides the appropriate knowledge environment; 14% remain undecided, whereas 9% do not share this opinion (strongly disagree and disagree); 68% agree (strongly agree and just agree) that classic agglomeration benefits (input-output relations and the local labour market), present in a cluster, are crucial for advancing its digital transformation; 23% remain undecided, whereas 9% do not share this opinion (strongly disagree and disagree). Fixed institutional dimension gives some 'luxury' for long-term planning and facilitates meaningful actions, as it offers a long-time perspective; 80% agree (strongly agree and just agree) that institutions and professional policy support available in a cluster, facilitate digital transformation; 14% remain undecided, whereas 6% do not share this opinion (strongly disagree and disagree).

Table 6.1 Relative importance of selected elements of *industrial commons*

Cluster facilitates digital transformation thanks to industrial commons: *(from the most to the least relevant)*	*No. 1*	*No. 2*	*No. 3*	*No. 4*
Business relations (customer ties; supplier linkages)	13	12	6	1
Knowledge environment (competences, know-how and skills)	10	12	5	3
Policy support—institutions and professional management	4	7	18	3
All are equally important and should be provided simultaneously	8	0	2	15

Source: Results of the survey

Business relations (13), ahead of the knowledge environment (10), are regarded as the most critical (first place) elements of ICs. Eight respondents see, first and foremost, all components as equally important.

The Importance of RV in HAv

Cluster Composition

By mapping the profiles of activities of entities located in HAv—its members—against the NACE classification, it can be diagnosed which sectors, in particular, they are representing (https://ec.europa.eu/eurostat/documents/3859598/5902521/ks-ra-07-015-en.pdf). These are the manufacture of air and spacecraft, and related machinery; repair and maintenance of aircraft and spacecraft; air transport; and activities, such as telecommunications; computer programming, consultancy and related events, or information service activities; as well as architectural and engineering activities; technical testing and analysis, and scientific research and development. Hence, the division, groups and classes of NACE present in HAv are various, implying a certain level of diversification, in fact, not only related, but also unrelated, which might be attributed to the significant, metropolitan, city character of this particular cluster.

According to the members' directory, there are 174 HAv members, which can be divided according to their form of the organisation into Research and Development, Production and MRO, Engineering Services, Other Services, Education and Training and Institutions/Associations. They represent different fields of activity.

Table 6.2 HAv composition according to field of activity (February 2019)

Fields of activity	
Aircraft Production and MRO	11
Aircraft Systems and Components	33
Structural/Mechanical Engineering	26
Manufacturing and Process Technology	36
Cabin Equipment	42
IT	19
HR Services	38
Consulting	56
Urban Air Mobility	9
Air Traffic Systems and Air Traffic Control	6

Source: Own elaboration based on HAv members directory available on www.hamburg-aviation. de/en/members.html (February 2019)

HAv represents two aspects of the aviation industry—activities linked to aerospace technology and engineering, construction and production of cabin systems, as well as the broad spectrum of services related to aeronautical technics and air traffic. The technological focus of the cluster members is much more extensive than the cluster concept and covers a heterogeneous field of knowledge-intensive services, from natural science to software development (Cantner, Graf & Töpfer, 2015). (CC9) 'To be honest, HAv is already pretty diversified. We have OEMs like Airbus or Lufthansa, we have consulting companies, we have small and medium-sized firms from different branches, IT, consulting, etc., but they all work, somehow, in the aviation industry'.

The diversification also happens at the level of single companies. For example, Airbus makes aerospace technologies adaptable in many different industries: thanks to additive manufacturing, they are becoming vertically integrated along the entire value chain, from design to serial production (Mellor, Hao & Zhang, 2014).

Complex Co-Creation

The specific need for co-operation, also in terms of collaboration with related sectors, derives from the aviation peculiarities, in particular, the complexity of the final product. Making an aircraft involves certainly more than solely manufacturing. It should be rather defined as an ITS of production, rich in accompanying services and data processing.

The feature of the civil aviation industry is its high degree of complexity that is embodied in the final product, which includes a wide range of components. (CS2) 'Aviation is about producing complex products, and it is tricky to assembly the final product'. Propulsion and navigation systems, which need to interact in the final product, are each extremely complex with a high dose of technological uncertainty pertaining to aircraft design (Buxbaum-Conradi, 2018). It requires advanced co-operation, if not co-creation. Co-creation refers to any activity, in which the consumer participates, actively and directly with the company, to design and develop new products, services and processes (Grabher & Ibert, 2018).

The regional aviation concept of 'specialisation' also seems strategically smart/clever. Even if not that technically advanced, cabin painting, fitting or interior design are not that research-intensive and knowledge abundant, the Hamburg offering is more frequently and quickly wearing off ('wear and tear'). It is depreciating and ageing relatively faster, and consequently, is more often in need of repair, causing a higher demand for local services.

A broader perspective is needed to assure the quality of the final product in the aviation sector. All partners, contractors, customers and suppliers should be involved in the 'production process' (co-creation). What matters in aviation is the total cost of ownership (TCO). It combines the price paid when buying the product and the following expenditures: future maintenance, fuel consumption and repair. TCO shows how much the owner would spend on an aircraft over the next few years. To calculate this TCO, one needs to know, not just the price of the purchased goods, but be familiar with the whole life cycle of the plane, to include all the following costs. Insight from users is critical. Short-term perspective does not pay off. It is crucial to have all partners under one roof, to account for possibly all aircraft stakeholders. (CR1) 'The saying in HAv goes—Airbus knows all the strengths, Lufthansa Technik knows all the weaknesses'.

Aircraft is an extremely complex product which requires the co-operation of various areas and input from many fields - the stronger the input connected to the final product, the better. (CC10) 'We are doing engines and need some insight from others. More co-operation across the chain would be interesting, because we always depend on other companies. We need a lot of suppliers, services; it would be easier if we are the one company, but it is impossible, obviously'.

The processes of manufacturing, slicing-up the previously promoted and implemented, thanks to modularisation and standardisation, have brought specific negative results. In this complex industry like aviation, interoperability of all components is critical, and dispersion and fragmentation cause problems with smooth integration. (CS2) 'In aviation, they have programmes (like A380, A320), so they are experimenting a bit; when working on something new, and you do not have standards, you have to meet, to share tacit knowledge'.

However, some tendency to re-integrate and to synthesise these dispersed activities can be observed. Experts agree that there are some frictions and iterations, but it seems that the value chain constellation is slowly changing. The consolidation trend ('growing together of OEM, trier 1, MRO firms') is also reflected in the new HAv strategy (55th HAv Forum, 2019).

(CE3) 'You obviously cannot collocate the complete value chain in one place, but the more integrated the system you put into the final product; the more it comes from collocated entities, who jointly develop and integrate it, the better'. It is duly advantageous that suppliers in HAv can interact that closely, while developing the final product, which is, in that case, the aircraft for the large contractor, Airbus. It does not mean the whole product needs to be produced within the cluster, but there needs to be some efficient communication processes within the cluster.

Balancing Diversification and Specialisation

The general findings of the interviews with respect to RV might be summarised as conditional balance. Cluster members and experts tend to agree that the right proportion of specialisation and diversification looks differently at various levels, from contrasting perspectives, and depending on the company's status and position in the value chain hierarchy. When at the cluster level, specific diversification is positive and brings more resilience, likewise in case of large firms (OEM or first-tier suppliers), the focused clearly defined specialisation should characterise small firms and further n-tier contractors. (CC5) 'In fact, the diversification depends on who you are in the hierarchy, if you are a system integrator. First or second-tier companies can afford diversification, but if you are a 3rd, 4th or 5th tier supplier, you simply need to be focused, to specialise in some narrow area'.

However, the servitisation of manufacturing, as well as progress in implementing I4.0 technologies, results in a growing number of firms with a diversified portfolio of products and services, offering quite universal horizontal solutions. The tendency of narrowly defined specialisation and clear division of task aligns with the accompanying trend of providing a broader portfolio of products and services, so, the 'diversification (with)in specialisation' co-exists with 'specialisation in diversification'.

For big companies, it is more common to look into other sectors. The need for a more diversified portfolio, with more diversification than specialisation, may seem top-down induced. It answers the many needs of local firms, in particular, those who are simultaneously members of both HAv and other Hamburg clusters. Such dual membership makes them prone to more cross-sectoral co-operation. The topic of co-operation matters, as for more general issues, there is always more interest among members to join forces. The more universal the aspect of potential collaboration, the higher the chance of success. It also holds for manufacturing firms, and in particular for SMEs, which might be more grateful and appreciate this top-down assistance than large firms, equipped adequately to fend for themselves. They seem to have recognised the needs and benefits of more diversification, some time ago. They have been enriching their portfolio or diverging toward some multi-utilities, also searching for solutions for their problems in related sectors.

Digitalisation is undoubtedly the challenge that intersects various industries, including aviation. Cluster experts see this trend as horizontal cross-sectoral issue spreading across different industries, and it is the task of cluster authorities to apply these mega societal changes, such as I4.0, or climate change, to work for all industries. As a result, it is equally important to hone the excellence in a given particular, often narrowly defined, industry; yet, at the same time, to seek collaboration across the sectors, along the defined megatrends like I4.0. Ultimately, there is a need to build the regional matrix—to cater to the needs of silos, the vertical industries, and to bind them horizontally, along joint topics.

The daily need to strike a balance between specialisation and diversification is not a general challenge for the cluster, as such. It is mirrored in its members' often SMEs, daily decisions. Codification of knowledge and modularisation processes, as implemented by Airbus, have influenced the relations with local firms. They found themselves needing to fit into the new structure of first-tier or second-tier suppliers. Some members have decided to focus on a particular field of expertise. Others have ventured in new areas and spread the specialisation. The local diversification within specialisation can also materialise via the processes of internal re-configuration and tendencies to share risk and responsibilities among OEM and first-tier contractors.

Within this explicit aviation specialisation, some internal diversification can be identified, mainly due to Airbus activities. There are three centres: CFK valley with lightweight specialisation in Stade, the main production facility in Hamburg Finkenwerde, and the EcoMat (Centre for Eco-efficient Materials & Technologies) in Bremen. The latter is focusing on material nanotechnology, AI, and covers all stages of an aircraft's life cycle, from research in new materials, to certification and production. There is consequently, some specialisation (a division of tasks) of these three places, which must link to Airbus's plans and projects. These techno-centres are nodes in Airbus's networks with their networks. It provides some heterogeneity and diversification, reflecting that slowly, the HAv cluster becomes more diversified and globally oriented. (CE2) 'Airbus seems to be like a spider in the web. It can sew the orientation, the directions'. In fact, this company decides about specialisation-and-diversification balance and distribution.

The complementary partners who bring corresponding abilities and skills are vital for clusters. (CC1) 'We offer software, conceptual design, system, programming, but need manufacturers, someone who does the hardware'. HAv companies tend to see more diversity as something positive. (CC3) 'It seems that earlier, HAv was more specific and focused, now it is getting more diverse, which is fine. Also, foreign firms are entering, and new companies bring their competences'. Obviously, each firm needs to be concentrated and focused on its own field of expertise. However, there also seems to be a natural need to integrate more from outside, as it helps to increase efficiency, adapt to market requirements, to be more competitive in the future.

(CC8) 'It is positive, to re-integrate more other related areas and activities, bringing all together'. As stressed by one firm, both specialisation and diversification are positive. On the one hand, companies need to concentrate on core business and sub-contracting certain activities, which are not strategic. On the other hand, the integration of activities helps achieve a specific size, which defines their position on the market.

There also clear voices that core competencies and specialisation define a cluster's competitive edge. (CC2) 'We know aviation, we know how a plane works, but also know the lighting. It makes sense to get insight from other fields, have a general overview from other sectors, but we should stay focused'. Some members even fear the de-focusing of activities, allowing the diversification, if any, then only in closely related areas. (CC12) 'I think in aviation, this specialisation is necessary, however, it is good to see how other industries are solving similar problems as well'.

As it seems, the list of HAv companies represents almost the whole value chain, with three big players and a lot of smaller companies—first, second, and subsequent tier suppliers. So, the activities comprise different technical specialisations, but also services like human resources, consulting or training. There are many highly specialised entities and some accompanying service providers. (CE3) 'There is no contradiction in it, that is still the aviation cluster'. Specialisation and diversification are therefore, not contradictory, but there is instead a clear division of tasks of different members within this aviation specialisation. Actually, both are important: specialisation and diversification have to be reconciled. It happens more easily in the case of horizontal technologies, which are not specific to one industry, and if one cluster can learn from another. (CC11) 'You need to find a fine balance. On the one hand, you need to be careful of staying too focused, to limit your focus on too few subjects; on the other hand, you should not spread it too widely, because you may end up fragmenting your attention, spreading resources too wide'. Clusters are well-advised to focus on the particular industry, but within that scope, they should try to cover as many different subjects as possible.

Branching and Spin-Outs

As it seems in the HAv case, it is not only entities representing related sectors who enrich the cluster with their activities, but also new related sub-specialisations can arise. These processes are further enhanced by branching and the emergence of new segments, like urban air mobility (UAM), including the unmanned aerial vehicles (UAVs). It is expected that following the current hype, the sustainable development of new sectors would materialise, which necessitates the development of appropriate infrastructure, provision of technologies and certificates, aerospace integration and social acceptance (HAv 55th Forum).

As noticed by one cluster expert, for many years, there were almost no new start-ups in aerospace. However, recently, also thanks to digitalisation, new ones are emerging and the more firms, the more positive are the network effects. ZAL, with co-ordinated projects (WinDroVe www.unternehmen-region.de/de/991992.php), supports co-operation across industries and the emergence of new areas like UAM. In fact, thanks to networking, many companies learned about that hidden potential. (CE4) 'They were unaware that many others are representing this field, and there is a chance for collaboration'.

Companies providing KIBS and representing other sectors, are enriching the HAv composition. (CE4) 'Recently, the new robot company—coming from the automotive industry, entered Hamburg'. It offers the proven solutions in the automotive industry, which can also be useful in the aviation sector, such as the new machine learning type or AI.

The digital connection of product, place and production alters the production chain and offers the possibilities to combine the components in multiple ways. It results in a cluster that is diversified from its aerospace origins to the wind turbine industry, as well as shipbuilding and automotive engineering (Menzel & Buxbaum-Conradi, 2018).

New sub-sectors can merge grounded in local competences. Lightweight industry followed a strategy of emancipation and differentiation. As a result, a spin-off cluster, the CFK Valley e.V., has emerged (Buxbaum-Conradi, 2018; https://cfk-valley.com/en/association/club/). It was founded in 2004 in Stade, primarily through the initiative of the locally-based Airbus group. It has some 30 years of CFRP (carbon fibre-reinforced polymer) experience. It counts more than 100 selected regional, national and international companies and institutes, with expertise covering the entire value chain of the high-performance, fibre-reinforced composites. Adopted in 2015, Strategy explicitly states 'diversification, internationalisation, regional value creation and training' as its significant goals.

One of the innovative flagship projects run in HAv is GROLAS a ground-based landing gear system. This is disruptive technology, enabling aeroplanes to land without the undercarriage, which could save around 20% of fuel. This would revolutionise the whole of aviation, but it will take time to get there. There is still lobbying and the interests of many traditional suppliers and manufacturers, preferring classic configurations. (CC1) 'They will not change unless they are forced to, for instance, due to environmental requirements'. Another new project with the HAv office as the project leader, is REALISE (www.realise.aero), which stands for runway, independent, automatic, land and launch system. It reflects the first stage of 'realisation', as well as the need to realise the potential behind it. It acknowledges the disruptive innovativeness of this technology and also the readiness of the whole concept.

HAv is not only developing new, genuinely innovative products like the ones mentioned above, but also moving or *stretching* into related areas, such as air urban mobility or UAVs. Some firms are already involved in work on UAV-drones. They have been developing a minimum viable product (MVP), which can already satisfy customers and provide feedback for future product development.

HAv experts stress that aviation has been developing for centuries, and it is impossible to make any further progress by merely ignoring the past decades of achievements. Instead, by building on it, in light of digital transformation, it is necessary to re-define the concept of mobility. (CS1) 'In the future, we will not talk just about the aviation, but broadly about mobility'. Future problems cannot be discussed and handled only within one industry. There is an obvious need to add other perspectives.

On a Final Note

Moving into new areas, branching into innovative related fields of activity (UAM) or even developing new market segments, like the cases of the REALISE project or GROLAS innovation show, require intensive and extensive co-creation (Redlich, Moritz & Wulfsberg, 2019; Prahald & Ramaswamy, 2004; Vargo, Maglio & Akaka, 2008). These ideas would not have been possible, if it had not been for the close interactions between different actors (B2B)—airport, aeroplane manufacturer or airlines.

The results of an anonymous online survey among cluster experts and cluster firms revealed that 54% agree (strongly agree and just agree), that the entrepreneurial ecosystem necessary for successful digital transformation, is provided in the cluster; 32% remain undecided, whereas 14% do not share this opinion (strongly disagree and disagree).

The co-opetition processes diagnosed in HAv—co-operation spaces when there are common interests, as well as legitimate and stimulating competition spaces when necessary (Drewello, Bouzar & Helfer, 2016)—resemble the concept of the fractal company. The results of the online survey revealed that 68% agree (strongly agree and just agree) that I4.0 introduces new business models with co-operating and competing units, and the cluster embodies such interactions; 23% remain undecided, whereas 9% do not share this opinion (strongly disagree and disagree).

The co-creation mentioned above implies vanishing boundaries among entities and stimulates the development of a connected company. The survey results showed that 60% agree (strongly agree and just agree) that I4.0 embodies the concept of 'connected enterprise' (blurred firms' boundaries), and the cluster reflects this concept; 26% remain undecided, whereas 14% do not share this opinion (strongly disagree and disagree).

Blending Processes in HAv

Bridging and Cross-Clustering

HAv managers, like the offices of other Hamburg clusters, strive to build bridges among them and create what Fromhold-Eisebith (2017) call 'clusterspace'.

In Hamburg, each sector is organised in a cluster (Figure 6.1). There are altogether eight clusters, which meet all necessary criteria and proper cluster definition epitomising the triple helix. The benefits obtained when clusters work together across their disciplines, made the EU back the concept of cross-clustering. In late 2014, Hamburg was selected as one of six model regions for modern cluster policy. Since then, all of Hamburg clusters' stakeholders have been involved in developing cross-clustering, guided by the overarching purpose to make better use in the future of the potential for innovation and added value that is available, thanks to the thematic intersections between Hamburg's clusters. It has been designated as 'cluster bridges' (www.hamburg.de/wirtschaft/clusterpolitik-modellregion).

These eight Hamburg metropolitan clusters have their specific path development. As stressed by the CRs (CR1, 3, 6 and 7), 'Here, in Hamburg, segments are different, and we may have little touchpoints. Hence, it is certainly easier when we discuss topics, which are common to all. We can talk "eye-to-eye", but indeed, as settings and scenarios we are in, are so different, it is often difficult'.

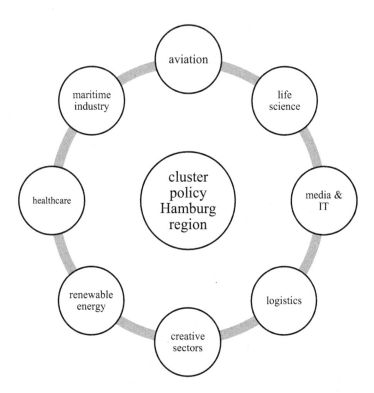

Figure 6.1 Hamburg clusters

Source: Own elaboration based on www.hamburg.de/wirtschaft/clusterpolitik-modellregion

The Ministry of Economy decided to bridge them and set up a platform of co-operation, which seems critical in the digital revolution. The co-learning space (www.co-learningspace.de) might prove vital in the I4.0 era, as it encourages co-operation across clusters—technologies applied in aviation, are also used in health, maritime, and so on. These meetings also aim at developing specific solutions for future joint problems (e.g. travelling of the elderly in 2030). (CS1) 'We create a person—a fictional character— grandpa Willi. We develop a story of an 85 year-old grandpa, who is visiting hi grand-daughter in Paris, and he faces many challenges. The question arises, how do we get him there? We adopted a holistic approach to using our strengths, to solve transformation problems'.

I4.0 instruments and technologies facilitate bringing clusters together. They are acting like a glue which binds them, a common thread of interest for representatives of various clusters. I4.0 solutions support the development of RV (aerodynamic wings—new in planes, have also been adopted in windmills, where the blades now resemble the plane wings with this curve upward), but also *unrelated variety* (c.f. elderly travelling).

Clusters in Hamburg are very autonomous, very different, so they need proper cluster management. Co-learning (an official project funded jointly by the state—Ministry 50% and European Commission 50%) is done in a pre-established format. Co-operation takes place formally via a weekly meeting of middle- and lower-level officers, and monthly, when higher-ranking representatives like CEOs and directors meet and discuss. When there are differences of opinion and some disagreement, it is easier to handle, thanks to this unique cluster fabric—trust and understating, plurality and mutual commitment. Thus, the cluster management needs to offer the ecosystem, which can facilitate such collaboration. It may seem to be of less importance for delivering concrete solutions, but it constitutes the necessary starting point for any further co-operation. Building trust, developing some code of conduct, sometimes, simply to get to know each other requires that stage-setting and preparations.

It should be mentioned that all these initiatives to learn from each other, thanks to the co-learning space and regular meetings in established format, help also to boost international expansion across industries (e.g. events on how to do business in Japan). So, *blending* (internal cross-industry co-operation) might lead towards and facilitate expansion abroad (i.e. *hubbing*); the overlap of these two processes materialises.

Cross-clustering happens, not only within the region, but takes place also on the national level. The Federal Ministry for Economic Affairs and Energy has been supporting the cross-cluster partnerships within the framework of 'Go cluster' initiative (www.clusterplattform.de/CLUS TER/Redaktion/EN/Downloads/Publications/cross_cluster_success_stories. pdf?__blob=publicationFile&v=7). HAv took part in such a project under the motto, 'Chemical and aviation industry on a common path'. It is rightly argued that chemical products offer diverse applications in aerospace. So far, mainly the perceived 'distance' between chemical suppliers and industrial OEM, the lack of transparency in value chains, as well as regulatory hurdles, prevent smooth co-operation between the chemicals and aviation industries. Nevertheless, the Aviation Cluster, Hamburg, and Chemie-Cluster, Bayern, are committed to a merger between their respective industries, which, however, requires the ability of 'thinking outside the box'.

Cross-cluster collaboration on a national level also materialises via co-operation with Silicon Saxony (Energy Efficient Aviation Solution [EEAS], BMBF). All these initiatives are in line with recent EU Commission plans to marry clusters—to form meta-clusters.

Projects (cross-clustering/*blending*) with Saxony or a Chemical cluster in Bayern have officially been completed with some follow-up co-operation most likely. Although, currently, no new projects of this type have been conducted; if some interest existed, HAv would be ready to start a new collaboration. Relatively low demand for such partnerships (cross-sectoral, nation-wide) might result from the perceived high entry barriers, as other sectors' firms may see high hurdles in starting a business in the aviation industry. The requirements concerning qualifications or certifications may deter other industries from such co-operation. Nevertheless, more players come, thanks to digitalisation, than would have been the situation in the past; more digital companies enter the aviation cluster.

Problem-Solving and the Universal Nature of I4.0

The process of sectoral expansion would benefit more from adopting the problem-oriented approach. Gathering members around a particular challenge, which is shared by them, facilitates the co-operation among sectors. It is further accelerated by the universal nature of many of the I4.0 technologies, which can, in fact, bind more easily the related sectors and act as a bridge for RV.

HAv has recommended the setting up and implementing of a development platform. It seems to be a useful tool for collaboration among cluster members. Nevertheless, in the beginning, it was welcomed with much suspicion and scepticism. This platform, however, proves to be the right way to increase business efficiency, which is of utmost importance for small and medium firms. (CC1) 'We met and spoke for two days on some topics; this close exchange allowed a better intervention, early correction if necessary, to improve the efficiency'. Many of the HAv innovative solutions are, in fact, general-purpose technologies (GPTs), which can facilitate further expansion in related sectors. (CC2) 'We provide aircraft cabins with human-centred lighting solutions, to positively manipulate an inner clock, so a human can shift easily to other time zones. You can have it in the car, on the ship, but you need it most in the aircraft'.

As put by one cluster expert, the only way to make the local players work together, is to agglomerate around some issue, in order to solve a specific challenge. Collaboration among sectors should happen naturally, come from the business itself, be initiated and implemented by focal players, interested in such co-operation. What can help, however, is a problem-oriented approach. When actors share the same problem or when they face similar difficulties, they are inclined to search for common solutions. (CS2) 'Solving real problems helps, not artificially aggregating actors'.

Innovation can happen in new creative digital industries, but also in old traditional ones. Often new ideas are useless, unless put into the actual process or unless applied in a real product. There seems to be too much hype about purely creative digital, thus the need to bring them down-to-earth, to adopt into classic areas, such as the food industry, aviation, maritime, and so forth. Different formats help to open the minds of local clusters. They aim at strengthening this cross-fertilisation like brainstorming sessions, world coffee roundtables stimulating creative thinking. (CO1) 'Groups are set at different tables, dedicated to a certain topic-problem, and they rotate, they think about what the previous group came up with, they change and modify it; in a way, they are jointly learning'. It is not merely a discussion detached from real problems; it is about solving these challenges.

Complementarity

In the opinion of cluster actors, the *blending* and adding of related sectors, should be regarded in terms of addressing the growing need for complementary competences. The sectoral expansion and more diversity in the aviation sector, should duly follow the principle of complementarity, which can then translate into a better defined and more sustainable competitive advantage.

More diversification, more RV or *blending*, in fact, might turn critical for cluster coherence, and its sustainability in the future, as it can mitigate and neutralise the direct competition.

Cluster firms are well aware of the risk of sharing knowledge with rivals, but admit that in such interactions, they can benefit as well, due to the access to complementary competences. There are two sides of this cluster symbiosis. (CE2) 'In a way, you search to collaborate not with direct competitors, but those with complementary skills and competences'. (CC3) 'New companies entering HAv, are very much close to the I4.0. We see this process going on; before there have been very specific aerospace companies and products, the new ones joining are very diverse and bring capabilities from other industries'.

Many companies agree that, particularly for small firms, it is beneficial to diversify in terms of bringing new skills, new corresponding supplementary competences. (CC1) 'The bigger the cluster diversification, the bigger the chance you will find someone with complementary capacities'. There is some emerging consensus that, on the one hand, what is needed is a focus on core activities and specialisation, on the other hand, bringing and integrating new businesses, which create a competitive advantage in the future.

Blending, as seen by cluster firms, results from digital transformation, as it implies changes in business models, moving away from merely manufacturing simple pieces of hardware to adding services, data processing and other features.

On a Final Note

There was the public local government initiative to set up the co-learning space with the aim of fostering cross-cluster co-operation. It brings value and supports the development of RV, but also *unrelated variety*. Clusters have regular meetings when they initiate R&D co-operation or have common training around topics, such as AI. The idea of inviting new players to the cluster (like leasees, but also including new, related sectors) or the approach to see the HCAT as training and educating, not just for the aviation industry, but rather as a centre of advanced schooling, as diagnosed in a new strategy (55th HAv Forum, 2019) indirectly confirm the relevance of RV and *blending* processes.

Clusters can display long-term growth, if they can maintain diversity, and that technological heterogeneity plays a central role in cluster evolution (Menzel & Fornahl, 2010).

The results of an anonymous online survey among cluster experts and cluster firms revealed that 57% agree (strongly agree and just agree) that digital transformation promotes cluster diversification—less sectoral specialisation; 29% remain undecided, whereas 14% do not share this opinion (strongly disagree and disagree).

Governments and public authorities assume responsibility in the implementation of the best business environment for firms to thrive (Tinguely, 2013). For this cluster policy, however, to be successful in the long run, the government would need to leverage the power of the technology gatekeepers—in particular, design the policies in a way, which allows gatekeepers to translate government objectives into meaningful objectives for themselves (Vernay, D'Ippolito & Pinkse, 2018; Jungwirth & Mueller, 2014). Cluster policies need to solve co-ordination problems among the cluster members, by creating safety in a highly uncertain world, however, without being captured by any group of interests (Duranton, 2011; Cantner, Graf & Töpfer, 2015). At the same time, any evaluations of cluster policies should not rely on aggregated statistics that ignore cluster-specific impact (Elola, Valdaliso, Franco & López, 2017).

The results of an anonymous online survey among cluster experts and cluster firms revealed that 77% agree (strongly agree and just agree) that cluster is an instrument of a modern industrial policy promoting the digital transformation; 14% remain undecided, whereas 9% do not share this opinion (strongly disagree and disagree).

Hubbing Strategy of HAv

Multi-Scalarity of Expansion

Geographical expansion takes place in HAv at different levels. Openness and co-operation with external partners are supported. Nevertheless, HAv members must belong to the metropolitan region, and a local footprint (office and regular clients) is required. The *stretching* of HAv is highlighted in the metropolitan area of Hamburg with, e.g. Airbus facilities in Finkenwerder, Stade and Buxtehude.

HAv has a formalised strategy which also focuses on internationalisation. The HAv office provides support services, enabling its members to access the EU internal market and third countries' markets and helps with the promotion of activities (marketing/visibility) and participation in international co-operation. Central target regions considered are Brazil, Canada, Japan and the United States, but this list could also include: France, Italy, Portugal, Spain and the United Kingdom. Besides, it assists members in participation at missions, events, study visits or international fairs.

As internationalisation becomes more and more critical for the German aviation industry, HAv initialises a series of workshops to develop a common strategy with all cluster members, including experts from ZAL. The first workshop yielded seven prospective regions for potential collaboration. In 2016, HAv signed a co-operation agreement with the aviation cluster in Montreal at the Farnborough International Air show. During the second Internationalisation Strategy Workshop, it highlighted two additional target regions (out of the selected seven) for future co-operation: Evora/Lisbon and San José dos Campos/Sao Paolo. As part of the 'Hightech Strategy', BMBF is funding this internationalisation process of the aviation industry in Hamburg. The co-operation with Portugal, Brazil and Canada builds on the restrictive rules and must meet specific, clearly defined criteria (www. bmbf.de/en/internationalisation-of-leading-edge-clusters-forward-looking-projects-and-comparable-1416.html). Foreign partners must respect the intellectual property rights and related standards. They need to act, according to the code of conduct, provide funding on an equal footing and the necessary complementary competencies (know-how and professional management). It is worth mentioning that a corresponding instrument has accompanied this programme—so-called 'learning measures' aimed at facilitating the sharing of best practices, gaining more knowledge from the execution of the primary, international co-operation projects.

To bolster the industry's position in a joint effort, HAv has initiated and now co-ordinates the European Aerospace Cluster Partnership (EACP). It started in 2009 with 24 European aerospace organisations in 11 countries, within the framework of CLUNET, a PRO INNO EUROPE project. In 2013, the EACP was recognised by the European Commission as one of 13 European Strategic Cluster Partnerships (ESCP). Since then, it has grown to include over 43 members from around 18 countries (www.eacp-aero.eu/about-eacp/member-chart.html). The EACP operates in an open and de-centralised way, building upon a set of continuous working groups, temporary consortia and bi- or multilateral ad-hoc partnerships (www.eacp-aero.

eu/about-eacp/mission.html). It is involved in various often EU-funded projects and programmes (Canape, EuroSME, Abroad and BeAware), which are linking various members in different constellations (www.eacp-aero.eu/projects.html). It aims to improve the global competitiveness in Europe, through intense inter-cluster collaboration. The EACP is regarded as an arena for mutual idea exchange among industry representatives, and a launch-pad for transnational aviation projects. As stipulated, the EACP should become a key contact point for the European Commission, with respect to all aviation issues. This co-operation fits into the inter-cluster alliances (ICAs), which is a nascent research field (Goerzen, 2018). Cluster managers, by striking the ICAs, allow the cluster boundaries to become more porous. In this way, they facilitate the flow of knowledge, reducing the liability of unconnectedness felt, particularly by SMEs (Baum & Oliver, 1991). Therefore, cluster management offering ICA provides an essential boundary-spanning function for resource-poor SMEs. It helps SMEs, who are pursuing the internationalisation and innovation to get access to people and pipelines. As HAv representatives argue, this increased internationali-sation is translated into more 'emancipated' stronger SMEs, better equipped for negotiating with outside partners in the future.

Worldwide co-operation and partnerships are conducted under the motto: 'a strong cluster needs strong allies'. Aside from the EACP, HAv main-tains national and international partnerships and co-operates with clusters from other industries in Hamburg, along with other leading-edge clusters and aviation clusters throughout Germany. The framework labelled Supply-Chain Excellence Initiative (SCEI) gathers representatives of German air transport associations or clusters' initiatives and works with the federal gov-ernment, Länder (states) and industry, with the aim to strengthen Germany's global competitiveness in this area (www.german-aerospace.de). The scale and speed of structural challenges faced by the aerospace industry put tradi-tional supplier relationships along GVCs under pressure. In some respects, the German supplier industry is at risk of losing a competitive advantage. Hence, SCEI, which aims at active development of stable and agile sup-ply chains at all value-added steps. Likewise, 'Aviation meets Chemistry' or metropolitan bridging (local cross-clustering) might be regarded as a prominent example of inter-clustering (Franco & Esteves, 2020; Cusin & Loubaresse, 2018; Lorenzen & Mudambi, 2012 Goerzen, 2018).

Region Plugged Into Global Networks

There is specific *hubbing* via Airbus linkages to France, UK or Spain. The relations within the group are best epitomised by the co-opetition; particu-larly with relation to Toulouse Aviation a major partner, and also, a larger one. (CR1) 'There is some jealousy, some co-operation, joint division of tasks and work'. So, *hubbing* happens via Airbus first-tier (direct co-operating) and second-tier (indirectly) partners. A clear division of labour with simultaneous co-operation between the two sides has been established over the last decades (Buxbaum-Conradi, 2018).

(CC9) 'As you have globally just a few aviation hubs, they are more or less somehow already together. So, there is, in fact, already international collaboration existing. If we are talking about digital transformation and more connected supply chains then, of course, digital transformation is a tool of more international openness'.

Thanks to Airbus, the whole region is 'plugged' into GVCs/GPN. Nevertheless, regional production networks are also embedded in broader systems of exchange relations that span clusters and go beyond the governance structures that are used to explain inter-firm linkages in global value chains (Bathelt & Li, 2014). Particularly impressive is the nature of these external relations that link different places and the knowledge circulation among them.

Buxbaum-Conradi (2018) stresses that Airbus-induced codification and the transformation of knowledge infrastructure during the modular transition affect the dynamics of GPN and the inter-relations between global and local developments. The case of Airbus modernisation and the consequences it has had for HAv, best epitomise how transformations, in the knowledge infrastructure of a production system, affect knowledge and production relations in a local industry cluster. HAv have experienced these processes of dis- and re-embedding of production and knowledge relations, as well as tensions and new challenges for local suppliers.

As argued by Buxbaum-Conradi (2018), cluster policies have over-emphasised the importance of local relations, whereas too little attention has been paid to better nesting within global knowledge relations. These developments have revealed that experience and know-how accumulated locally over decades become simply obsolete, due to more flexible strategy of sourcing engineering services. Digitalisation is also a possibility with which to advance international expansion. New business ideas and strategies come up, and they force companies to look internationally to connect with the outside world.

SMEs Liability of Unconnectedness and Emancipation

The cluster role in the processes of internationalisation cannot be over-estimated, given the dominance of SMEs suffering the liability of unconnectedness. Participation in international projects, thanks to the door-opening by HAv managers, also leads to small companies' emancipation vis-a-vis other large players. It makes them more immune and reduces their over-dependence. Airbus dominates all the linkages. Nevertheless, there is a tendency that suppliers, once they are internationalised, become more empowered and emancipated. Once they become attractive for other companies (like Boeing), the perception and attitude of Airbus will change as well, so it cannot dictate and dominate the relationship that easily. So, the internationalising makes firms—n-trier suppliers—more attractive, more equal; reducing the members' asymmetry.

Internationalisation efforts are essential from the perspective of SMEs, which lack their own resources and capabilities to venture abroad; so, it is relevant to provide them with insight about the foreign market and streamline the access to distant contractors. However, this happens slowly, and it is hard to see the results, to evaluate the effects of such activities. (CO1) 'International activities improve the external visibility and improve publicity and, in fact, are important, but how they translate into actual internationalisation of cluster members remains unknown and is tough to be measured'. (CE3) 'I have observed these activities for some time, and I think for some entities, located here in Hamburg, it is a quite interesting development, because of the danger of the consequences of relying so much on Airbus'. Intensive relations with one large company, in that case, SMEs around Airbus, bring the risk of over-dependency. *Hubbing*, the expansion of international relations, can in this respect, be seen as risk reduction, diversification which leads to more immune SMEs and more resilient to possible negative shock resulting from over-dependency. It opens for the SMEs new avenues, other customers which they can link to, or other aviation clusters. It also implies that many foreign delegations visit Hamburg. (CC5) 'HAv can open markets for SMEs'.

However, companies seeking to develop international ties often face resource constraints. Many small firms acknowledge the internationalisation efforts by HAv. (CC12) 'We are looking forward to having more internationalisation'. Nevertheless, they often do not have the resources to fully exploit available opportunities. They are under-staffed and cannot dedicate more time and energy to get engaged.

Transnational co-operation is rather beneficial, but each firm must decide and check if this fits into its strategy. Such an approach suggests a need for a firm-level granular perspective. (CC6) 'Benefits are conditional on which role you play'. Small firms admit that building relationships, thanks to HAv internationalisation efforts, is like the first step to find out more and (CC3) 'pave the ground for future relations, when we are bigger'. In general, even if not right now up and running, these activities create basis for future relations.

(CC1) 'If we had been interested, we could have participated. However, so far, we have not benefitted much, we simply did not need to. We are in the early stage of co-operation with some foreign companies; more at the technology development/research stage. Later, when it comes to marketing, commercialisation, perhaps, we will use this opportunity'.

Firms agree these are often only first steps, but some commercial co-operation might emerge out of these meetings, discussions and getting to know each other.

There are, however, also sceptical voices raised. (CC8) 'I am not sure if this activity will benefit SMEs. Many operate very locally. These are local service providers. It is extremely difficult to access other markets, which are closed, have their own set-up of firms, suppliers'.

HAv members admit that the whole aerospace community is getting much more open and international. (CC7) 'If I think back 20 years ago, it was merely Airbus. When I look at the market right now, we are working with Chinese firms and other players'.

Nature of International Relations and I.40

Industry 4.0 allows HAv members to work more internationally and to co-operate with other international aerospace hubs and hotspots, like Montreal, Seattle or Toulouse. Skype and all modern ICT tools enable distant communication. However, it matters to meet, to have face-to-face contacts; as co-operation with Canada proves (joint meetings at least twice a year). Digitisation stimulates *hubbing*, facilitates communications with external partners, for instance within the EACP, and reduces the costs of distant collaboration, controlling, and so on. However, besides regarding I4.0 solutions as (1) instruments, they can also be perceived in terms of (2) knowledge— adopting foreign solutions from outside; like borrowing know-how from leaders (USA) and learning from them.

R&D international relations, fostered in HAv, also aim to develop new platforms of co-operation (like after the A350 expires). However, this encompasses, not only R&D projects, but also works on supply chain, and recently, HR co-operation. It has been initiated to grasp more knowledge of how to deal with upcoming digital challenges on the labour markets—how to train, re-qualify and which courses to offer.

HAv has an international strategy, but not in terms of attracting foreign investment. For instance, with Canada, the target is to enter new research projects. The innovative research co-operation is meant as the first stage; later, the second or third phases would be dealing with discovering market opportunities; and investment, perhaps, can come at the end. HAv focuses on B2B, seeks to help the companies to learn about market possibilities and provide them with contacts. (CR1, 3, 6 and 7) 'We do not have specific competences, but can connect people, act as a matchmaker, to help other firms to connect with local companies, and one day, they might want to invest here'.

The international expansion encompasses various co-operation forms with partners around the globe. Whereas partnerships with Canada, Portugal and Brazil are the most prominent ones, collaboration with the UK (also recently strengthened, due to uncertainty arising from Brexit) or Japan is progressing. Usually, HAv helps and assist firms in the exploratory first phase of the collaboration, facilitating matchmaking, assisting delegations of businesspeople, providing information on mutual investment possibilities. However, there is no explicit aim to increase the exports of local firms, or their investments abroad, or to attract explicitly more firms to the region. It might be one of the goals and side effects of international partnerships, but it is not featuring high on the agenda. This might also be the result of the peculiarities of the aviation industry, where instant re-location and swift export/import investment decisions are rare. International expansion in this industry is more about the right plugging-in of the global production networks, about establishing network and value chains relations. (CR1, 3, 6 and 7) 'Aviation is dominated by a few large firms, like Boeing or Airbus, so here, there is less a question of where to relocate, but rather what region fits best into my current project, my needs? We create opportunities to bring projects; we have to be match-makers'. Hence, HAv's role is not to specifically increase exports or foreign investments, which is, more directly, the task of Hamburg Invest Agency (https://en.hamburg-invest.com).

Sustainability

The significant challenge, in terms of geographical expansion, lies in the sustainability of these new relations. (CS2) 'In all these international projects, usually knowledge is being exchanged, but the problem is the sustainability of such collaboration. How to sustain this often, unfortunately, superficial co-operation, which tends to die soon after the funding stops'.

Indeed, it helps to attract other outside firms, to present the Hamburg region like a magnet, an attractive region to invest. However, there is a need to build the bottom-up strategy, which would reflect and internalise the needs of members, not to be imposed top-down. (CO1) 'We do not have any measurement, indicators which would be used to assess the impact of international activities on real cluster members performance, but with clusters, it is extremely tricky to capture such processes, to give concrete figures. In fact, the same can be said with other indicators like patents—they often say little about true innovativeness, as they are applied and granted to be hidden from competitors; to be rather kept in the drawer and not applied as innovations. Therefore, using such indicators might be misleading. One has to be careful with handling such measurement'.

There is a growing perception that to be more competitive, firms need to bring fresh ideas from outside. It is essential to connect to the outside world and source from international partners. However, as argued by one expert, first, it is necessary to develop and enhance local strengths. (CE2) 'Endogenous growth comes first, and internationalisation can act as a facilitator of this growth, not aim per se'. Internationalisation must come from focal players, must be embedded here in the cluster and reflect local needs.

Both the B2B, as well C2C contacts are desired, as firms argue that a cluster needs to have partnerships, with other clusters elsewhere. HAv initiate the partnerships with their peers abroad, within the BMBF project, which fits into the concept of internationalisation regarded as C2C co-operation. The area of collaboration and list of possible partner clusters is, however, always the result of previous joint discussions and negotiations with HAv stakeholders. The EACP co-ordinated by HAv, and pooling more or less selected and established clusters, is tasked with facilitating the joint application and conduct of the EU-funded projects. It aims to secure a more stable future for cluster members, while assuring the continuity of relations.

Cluster experts agree that internationalisation is a vital issue but stress the need to take care that it is a 'two-way street'. (CE4) 'It must not be a one-way street, that we provide and share our knowledge, and let, in that way, the competitors to get stronger at our expense. We do not want to train our competitors. It must be "win-win", that is why Canada has been selected and co-operation with Montreal as an equal partner—they can learn from us; we can gain something from them'.

The international partnerships, supported by the HAv, consequently, focus on creating this 'win-win' situation. It also implies that out of many (up to 15 annually) calls and demands to set up partnerships, only a few have materialised. A limited number of MoU signed, reflects the priority given to quality than quantity. (CR1, 3, 6 and 7) 'We have 10–15 international delegations, but are selective, focus more on quality, we signed only a few MoU, but indeed demand is high'. This approach aligns with the concept of alliance saturation and the negative consequences of reaching the upper limit of co-operation possibilities (Goerzen, 2018).

Brexit, in the eyes of some experts, as a kind of external shock, may influence the functioning of HAv, perhaps positively, if certain activities are relocated here from the United Kingdom. This suggests that external relations might go both ways and/or be reversed.

On a Final Note

These results confirm the relevance of networking for internationalisation processes, which has been recognised in the literature. In particular, it is the liability of outsiders to the network, which is the reason for uncertainty influencing the internationalisation engagement (Johanson & Vahlne, 2009; Richardson, Yamin & Sinkovics, 2012) negatively. Assistance offered in clusters is, as this study confirms, of highest importance for SMEs and start-ups experiencing the liability of unconnectedness (Baum & Oliver, 1991). The results of an anonymous online survey among cluster experts and cluster firms revealed that 66% agree (strongly agree and just agree) that digital transformation implies a more international openness of the cluster; 28% remain undecided, whereas 6% do not share this opinion (strongly disagree and disagree).

7 Summary of the Results

Overview

This volume addresses the issue of cluster transformation within digital transformation. It aims at answering the questions of how the cluster can deliver ICs and RV, and how it *stretches*?

Concerning the first problem, it might be argued that ICs are being developed in the HAv, by gradual and incremental accumulation of triple helix components. It happens by stimulating the critical mass of knowledge, business/industry activity and policy framework orchestrating and governing the cluster's members. It reflects Hidalgo's (2015) call that industry needs 'know-how', but 'know-how' needs business. Besides collecting components, it remains critical to safeguard efficient and effective relations between them hence, the activities of a middle-ground, organisation of fairs or exhibitions. In fact, the ZAL, likewise HECAS alone, might epitomise or incarnate the triple helix idea, as they present themselves as the interface of academia, business and administration. These local players are strongly and mutually intertwined, linked by various relations or often members within each other. It enables synergy and improves co-operation, reinforces the overall HAv mission and safeguards the coherent vision. Nevertheless, the downside of this situation is an intricate cobweb of relations, unclear status, with tensions, suspicions and rivalry beneath the surface.

Related variety, closely linked with technological diversification in the HAv, takes the form of covering the complete life cycle of an aircraft and the entire value chain of aviation. Provision of RV happens via mechanisms, allowing the free flow of 'know-how', the exchange of knowledge, by establishing linkages and connections between members and sectors they represent.

The *stretching* processes encompass both *blending* and *hubbing*. The latter in the HAv means opening up the cluster to the outside world, in particular, thanks to hosting members from outside, Airbus Toulouse/co-operation networks, activities of the EACP or strategic links with selected foreign clusters in Portugal, Brazil and Canada. *Blending* is also actively supported by combining bottom-up and top-down processes, in particular, by cross-clustering, co-learning and bridging initiatives of the Hamburg Metropolitan Region.

Given the current nature of production processes, the understanding of specialisation should be relaxed. The cluster reflects specialisation in an array of related industries (Delgado, Porter & Stern, 2015). As confirmed in the aerospace Basque cluster, RV can indeed positively contribute to the development (Elola, Valdaliso & López, 2013). Thus, results obtained, correspond with the previous claims that the theoretical notions of specialisation and diversification are too simplistic to capture the relationship between regional industry structure and economic growth (Content & Frenken, 2016). Based on the above, it might be argued that the HAv incarnates the *light* version of RV and *hubbing* process; that it provides the *semi-RV* and experiences some *semi-hubbing* (Figure 7.1).

I4.0 and Cluster Co-Relations

Although the HAv belongs to I4.0 German clusters, interviewees seem cautious whether it is indeed the case. They point out that I4.0 is in the

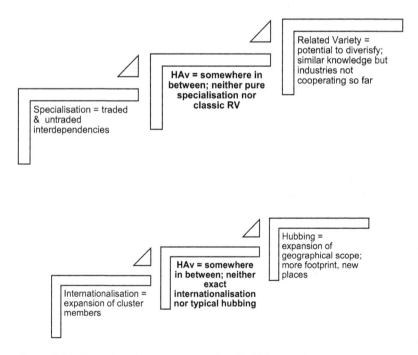

Figure 7.1 HAv against the concepts of RV and hubbing

Source: Author's own proposal

background of HAv's mission. It is a common thread of HAv's activities and acts as a modulator and factor of change. It is both an instrument and ingredient, facilitating modern aviation. 'Just' some technologies (cobots, digital twins and AI) are adopted, as human still matters in this sector. The cluster aims at raising the awareness of the digital transformation's related challenges and seeks to facilitate the critical HR developments, education and talent, as well as skills nurturing for the metropolitan region. As a result, the approach of HAv towards I4.0 might also be described as soft and much future-oriented. It is also clear that understanding of I4.0 varies among cluster entities, although, they are regarded mostly as highly innovative and representing advanced technologies.

Industry 4.0 could be more visible on HAv's agenda, resulting in the aim to raise awareness and teach members about the I4.0 impact on business (Bourke & Roper, 2019). Actions so far have been concentrated mainly on improving the knowledge about I4.0, illuminating the fact that I.40 is more than technologies, or engineering, as it requires a change of business models. Unfortunately, this aspect in general discourse seems to be neglected or rarely mentioned. The peculiarities of the aviation industry should be stressed and taken into account. This sector is much less susceptible to automation or digitised integration than the automotive industry, where thousands of cars leave the assembly line each day. A maximum one aeroplane a day can be manufactured. So, the whole production system and the business model look quite different, implying lower propensity or susceptibility to I4.0 solutions. The human role in this sector also means that new digital technologies play a complementary, rather than a substituting function, in the digitalisation of aviation. It is not that easy to automatise production of an aircraft, as in the car industry. (CR1–7) 'Here we can produce 30 of A320 per month (which gives, anyway, an impressive one aircraft per day), but when compared to the automotive sector, it is almost hand-made. We don't have modular production as in the car industry. It is a sequence. First, we build fuselage. Then, we do the cabin fitting, wiring. So, you need both humans and machines, it would be tricky to bring just robots; we have different settings here in aviation—it is a more supportive system with cobots, which complement the humans'.

Many companies are thinking about I4.0, but what is not common yet, is to see I4.0 as new business models, bringing new opportunities. The HAv office, therefore, concentrates on raising awareness about these new elements of I4.0 technologies. Local experts agree that they are at the beginning of this megatrend. Aerospace has very innovative sectors, although, only some of the I4.0 technologies have been applied so far. (CE2) 'Firms seem to continue picking up more topics from this megatrend, and flexibly follow the leaders like Airbus'. (CS1) 'There are also some real pioneers in I4.0, here in HAv, and there is a push to make more, to advance this in the cluster, and to diagnose the direction where to go'.

The cluster might become more diversified and less geographically con-centrated, but this, as seen by HAv representatives, happens, regardless of digital transformation. Growing international openness cannot, and will not, occur at the expense of local roots, regional embeddedness and iden-tity. Cluster changes—more diversification and less concentration—should also be perceived as the function of its constituent companies' modifica-tions. Thus, the cluster transformation digitally induced, i.e. the cluster transformation in digital transformation, derives from its members' trans-formation. Global processes and tendencies require new business models and new strategies; force to open and to diversify and cluster as such echoes this.

ICs, RV and Stretching in HAv

Based on the results of conducted qualitative studies, the following findings can be formulated:

- The provision of ICs, i.e. the bundling of knowledge, business and pol-icy, is embodied in the profile of HAv institutions. For instance, ZAL aims at being an interface of industry and science; at networking busi-ness, research and policy. It is further strengthened by simultaneous membership of these institutions in each other or by the co-ordinating role they play (ZAL for research, HECAS & Hansa Aerospace for sup-ply chain and HCAT+ for education). Business relations and network-ing more than expected, the knowledge exchange matters mostly for cluster members, in particular, SMEs, for which cluster membership confers legitimacy (Ferreira, Raposo, Rutten & Varga, 2014). Access to large players—being the centre of gravity—and to political con-nections, is also relevant in the eyes of many small members. Future skills feature high on the cluster agenda. Securing future competences is the task of both HCAT+—in terms of foreseeing and developing them, and ZAL—with regard to integrating and applying them. Pre-dicting and shaping future skills takes place in different dimensions. It is not only the above-mentioned specialised entities like HCAT+, but also dedicated programmes (DigiNet.air), regular training and events on skill development, and last, but not least, the local labour market with practices of job-hopping and post-switching possible, due to co-location and proximity. Anticipating future skills and delivering them is of utmost importance. At the same time, past developments, in par-ticular, the previously destroyed industrial fabric, which is hard to be re-instated, impact on the current provision of ICs. In fact, the main task for CO is exactly finding the *commons*; that what binds, what local

Table 7.1 Key variables of the analysis in the HAv cluster

Component/Process	Hubbing (geographical scale)	Blending (sectoral scope)
Industrial Commons = four universities, three big commercial players, research labs, initiatives and associations Three pillars: R&D moderated by ZAL; skills expertise moderated by HCAT+; SMEs supply chain by HECAS and Hansa Aerospace	Geographical expansion on different scales: • *region* = via members from outside (Lübeck) and plants in Buxtehude, Stade and Finkenverder, although always 'Metropolitan footprint'; • *National* = co-operation with DE aviation clusters—SCEI supply-chain excellence initiative; • *EU level* = Airbus, GVC links; Toulouse, direct/indirect • *Global* = EACP, New High-Tech Strategy of BMBF—Canada ✓ *proactive, purposeful, initiated by CO*	✓ *Often overlap with blending (e.g. 'Chemistry meets Aviation')*
RV = complete life cycle of aircraft and entire value chain of aviation = cabin fitting, aircraft, transport, MRO; aviation, aerospace, aeronautics	✓ *Overlap with hubbing (e.g. 'how to do business in Japan')*	• Co-learning space = cross-clustering among eight Hamburg clusters (renewable energy, health, maritime, etc.) • Meta-cluster co-operation nation-wide—e.g. with chemical industry ✓ *proactive, purposeful, initiated by CO*

Source: Author's own proposal

entities share. They need to take the commons outside the bracket as a glue for collaboration.

- RV in HAv derives from the fact that the region covers the complete life cycle of aircraft and the entire value chain of aviation; it encompasses aerospace, aeronautics and aviation, production and assembling, as well as MRO services. This co-existence and co-creation ('under one roof') are facilitated by the universal nature of I4.0 and profoundly impacted by the nature of the aviation industry. However, it is not only adding, i.e. the co-creation with partners, which enables the emergence of RV, but also the multiplication, i.e. the spin-out and development of new clusters. The role of relatedness reflects upon the matrix approach adopted, when the silos of vertical specialisation are linked via the universal cross-sectoral topics—societal megatrends in fact, like I4.0—the digital transformation. The RV of the HAv cluster derives from the balance between specialisation and diversification defined by its members.

- *Blending* builds upon the solving problem. Addressing jointly shared challenges seems to facilitate this sectoral expansion, which is also influenced by the universal, horizontal or cross-sectoral nature of I4.0 technologies. It happens, not only thanks to CO, and dedicated initiatives, such as co-learning and bridging or cross-clustering, but also by the spin-outs and new-born clusters. Successful *blending* requires finding the '*common*' and using it as a glue for all activities.

- *Hubbing* is a multi-scalar process, which is taking place at different levels and in different scales, from expanding the local footprint to concluding global partnerships. It should derive from actual cluster members' preferences and requires, particularly at the international level, efforts and mechanisms to be naturally sustained. It is also difficult to be measured with the results not easy to be adequately captured by any quantitative indices. For SMEs, suffering the unconnectedness liability, the assistance of CO in the internationalisation, acts as a 'door-opener'. However, it must also be noted that provided opportunities cannot often be exploited appropriately, due to resource constraints experienced by small firms, which creates some vicious circles.

- HAv actors reveal a sober approach towards *blending* and *hubbing*, as they stress the need for limited and cautious 'de-focusing' of activates, and strategic engagement with international expansion, mindful of the multiple risks involved.

The results obtained also highlight the previously identified aerospace industry attitude towards specialisation, as associated with risks of potential knowledge leakages (Speldekamp, Knoben & Saka-Helmhout, 2019). So, indirectly, they can confirm the possible detrimental effects of geographical specialisation (localisation economies), as well as confirming the capabilities of these companies to absorb spill-overs from other, sometimes unrelated industries. These observations lead to the identification of a particular pattern, whereby, the provision of IC and RV and processes of *blending* and *hubbing* are influenced by the moderating effects of industry (i.e. its propensity to I4.), key actors (size and power) and the universal nature of I4.0 technologies.

The co-learning initiatives, undertaken in Hamburg, seem to be an answer to the calls of adequate managing of knowledge networks in localities of learning (Brinkhoff, Suwala & Kulke, 2016). Although it is assumed that ICs are associated with *hubbing* processes mainly and RV develops chiefly thanks to the *blending* process, all these concepts share some commonalities. As the HAv case shows, *hubbing* and *blending* can overlap, i.e. happen simultaneously, whereas RV might be perceived as a sub-category of ICs. All in all, HAv seems to follow the presumed path of becoming more inter-regional and also cross-sectoral. While *blending*, i.e. the sectoral expansion, is indeed linked to the provision of RV (it seems difficult to absolutely decide which phenomenon reflects more—a process or the nature of cluster); the regional expansion, i.e. *hubbing*, does not seem to be contributing, particularly, to the development of ICs.

As the research followed the GTM, the main findings have been derived from the gradual iterative process of data collecting and analysing. First, the quotations 'in extenso' gathered during interviews and via informant centric insight, have been analysed and critically assessed. It has led to the creation of second-order constructs—the codes which summarise the insight and give a label to aspects raised by interviewees. These codes—grouped and re-phrased—become in the next stages, the properties of the key categories defined in this research (Figure 7.2). These four categories had been set in advance, which implies adopting the hybrid form of GTM.

In particular, by seeking to move 'beyond the inductive theory building towards the contextualised explanation' (Welch, Piekkari, Plakoyiannaki & Paavilainen-Mäntymäki, 2011), the provision of IC and RV and *stretching* processes in HAv can be diagnosed and explained.

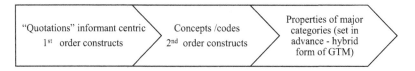

Figure 7.2 Procedure adopted—provision of IC and RV and *stretching* processes in HAv—GTM: from inductive theory building to contextualised explanation

Source: Author's own proposal

Peculiarities of Cluster and I4.0 Relations Diagnosed in HAv

Based on conducted interviews and in-depth study on HAv, the following research proposals and statements—grounded in empirics—can be advanced. They may serve as departure points for further, more quantitative or more nuanced studies, along with comparable research on other clusters (Figure 7.3).

- Provision of ICs is about predicting and jointly (*common*—taken outside the bracket as something which binds) developing future digital skills (as well as neutralising past mistakes—rebuilding a local manufacturing base). It is moderated by member size (asymmetry), industry's nature and its idiosyncrasies (entry costs; closed sectors, the propensity to I4.0 adaptation and the role of a human) and is conditional on communication culture, the level of competition and co-operation, as well as CO support. However, due to co-opetition and asymmetries of relations, the centripetal and centrifugal forces impact on the provision of IC. The time dimension with regard to the IC provision, features clearly in the HAv case—previous decisions (modularisation and offshoring leading to the destruction of local ties and disappearing industrial fabric) and future outlook (need to provide skills for next generations and anticipate future competences)—shape the local ICs.

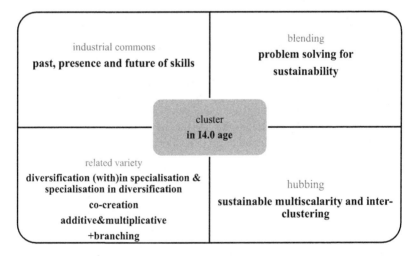

Figure 7.3 Key components of the analysis

Source: Author's own proposal based on the conducted study

Besides, the development of trust, which is critical for business relations and knowledge sharing, takes time. It confirms the time compression diseconomies (Dierickx & Cool, 1989). Cluster members tend to adopt a long-term perspective when entering into international projects (not blinded by the need for quick, short-term gains). Future skills, as a central element of IC provision should be common, shared by all members (owned by them), jointly developed and accurately communicated, which requires building trust and developing cluster identity. Nevertheless, the capability of the cluster, in terms of IC provision, in response to the I4.0 fashionable trend and against the background of the discourse advocating digital transformation should not be over-rated.

- *Related variety* draws on the co-creation processes, typically given industry's nature and co-learning, due to the universal character of I4.0. It can be seen as the sum of the members' balance between diversification and specialisation. RV, thanks to the universal nature of I4.0 solutions, is both additive (co-creation and influx of new activities, usually services, which reflects territorial servitisation) and multiplicative (spin-outs and emancipation of new specialisations). Besides, it implies venturing into new areas (UAV and UAM), creating nascent markets and branching. RV might be perceived as 'diversification (with)in specialisation' due to existing division of tasks, mainly guided by the Airbus network, but also as 'specialisation in diversification' given the portfolio of many members. The activities present in HAv reflect some clever specialisation, strategically covering almost the whole value chain, yet focusing on the later stages, and missing the most critical, in terms of I4.0 early phases of R&D. The uniqueness of aviation and inherent need of co-creation, also due to the guiding principle of total cost ownership (TCO), requires a broader perspective and necessitates the involvement of related sectors. Nevertheless, the universal nature of I4.0 technologies can serve as a bridge for the provision of RV.

- *Hubbing* can be described by multi-scalarity and sustainability. It takes place at different levels and ranges from metropolitan *stretching* to global institutional partnerships. It implies plugging-in international (aviation) networks. In order to ensure sustainability, it must be defined by members' preferences and be forward-looking. The uniqueness of aviation implies certain hurdles and barriers, which can deter co-operation. The openness which combines partnerships, projects at multiple levels, usually in institutionalised forms, should come together with internal galvanising. *Hubbing* can be seen as an over-dependency reduction leading to more 'one-large-player-dependant-caused-shock' immune SMEs. *Hubbing* can also, thanks to the C2C relations, exemplify the processes of inter-clustering (Lorenzen & Mudambi, 2012; Franco & Esteves, 2020; Cusin & Loubaresse, 2018; Schüßler, Decker & Lerch, 2013; Goerzen, 2018).

• *Blending* takes the form of local and national co-learning and bridging, facilitated by the universal nature of I4.0 and problem-solving orientation. However, it is hampered by the peculiarities of the aviation industry (oligopolistic nature or organisation around 'programmes'), which is perceived as a closed sector with high entry barriers and many hurdles. Adding new sectors and activities, the additive character of *blending* is accompanied by the multiplicative nature with emerging spin-outs/offs. Problem-solving seems critical for successful sectoral expansion. Problem-orientation helps, integrates naturally and fosters co-learning and cross-collaboration. *Blending* might prove vital for sustainability, as it can provide complementary competencies, defining the future competitive advantage of cluster members and the cluster, itself. In fact, as demonstrated by Montresor and Antonietti (2019), endowment in KETs—including some I4.0 technologies—may enable the complementarity and region's diversification, by stimulating the inter-chain upgrading, i.e. leveraging skills in other GVCs (Rehnberg & Ponte, 2018).

• Cluster in the digital age needs to reconcile specialisation and diversification. On the single company level, the specialisation should be the guiding principle; on the cluster level, the focus should be on some core competencies, which accommodate related areas (specialised firms). Finally, on the city/region level, there is a clear need and natural tendency of more diversification and cross-clustering.

• The HAv case allows diagnosing some specific trait of cluster evolution or a feature of *cluster 2.0*, i.e. the internal emergence of new offspring (sub)clusters. It happens via the process of establishing subfields of activity (sub-industry—Valdaliso, Elola & Franco, 2016), or territorially, as the case of CFK Valley or ZAL might suggest.

• The HAv case confirms that the cluster can be seen as an organising format for the implementation of I4.0 technologies, and the universal nature of I.40 is perceived as a common thread that binds different entities. I4.0 stands not only for BMI, but also implies that future manufacturing would be all about intelligent, interconnected technology systems.

• Industry 4.0, or digital business transformation, comes in many forms in local clusters, as the case of HAv shows, as developed technologies (knowledge), implemented solutions or anticipated and shaped skills. Due to various industries' I4.0 penetration or propensity, the intensity of I4.0 and I4.0 absorption may vary in each cluster. It is, nevertheless, a common thread of different activities factored in cluster functioning (resembling GPT or KET). It is one of the grand challenges and societal megatrends affecting the business organisation and also the clusters.

• I4.0's dynamic and complex nature emphasises the time dimension of provided IC, which needs to be future-oriented, anticipatory and forward-looking (not just offered, completed). Local co-opetition conditions, including the symmetry/dominance of some players, as well as communication and involvement of COs, play a role in the provision of such IC. It is a CO's duty to provide conditions, which enable cluster firms to leverage the cluster-based resources, effectively.

• The importance attached by CCs to the business relations and networking possibilities suggests that I4.0 implementation may be the result of a contagious process and mutual learning, observation or mimicking each other.

• Its (cluster net or total) RV would derive from the 'specialisation-diversification balance', as decided by each CC. The current profile of many of them (with a portfolio of different offer) proves that tendency (engineering solutions for aviation, automobiles; training and consulting for various related sectors). At the same time, the trend of 'diversification within specialisation' seems to be a common pattern among many firms from the Airbus network.

• The universal character of I4.0 technologies (GPT) makes the co-learning and knowledge exchange easier. It also derives from the problem-solving orientation, which these technologies enable and which can bind various sectors and industries. *Blending* can be seen as a natural complement to activities undertaken vertically within each industry and a necessary element of improving their competitiveness.

• Digital transformation or I4.0 is not only an instrument enabling distant collaboration and facilitating *hubbing* but is also such a topic and subject of this co-operation. This collaboration is multi-scalar, should reflect the cluster members' (geographical) preferences and requires systematic efforts to be sustained.

• Sectoral and geographical expansions—scale and scope changes—should be seen as part of cluster evolution (Njøs et al., 2017a, b). I4.0 is a megatrend affecting the cluster's existence, although, other incidental shocks should be mentioned as potential triggers for cluster re-organisation and change. The news announced on February 14, 2019, that Airbus would stop production of its Jumbo jet A380 in 2021 was sad, but a long-overdue announcement, and indeed, also a negative message, although, this might turn out to bring something positive to the cluster in the future, when adequately harnessed. Besides, it would be interesting to see how Brexit will affect the industry.

- Findings stress the need of a granular approach—the importance of focusing the lenses on a single firm's level. It is due to identified conditionality of specific elements or the benefits of certain activities. Depending on the company's size and its position, the gains from cluster *hubbing* can differ, likewise the benefits from diversification or progress in advancing the I4.0 implementation.
- It seems that most advantages named by cluster members and ascribed to HAv membership can be summarised as leading to increased efficiency and enhanced competitiveness. It corresponds with the results of numerous previous studies on 'cluster effects'. Interestingly, less attention and importance have been attached explicitly to the innovativeness, which might have been expected to feature more prominently in the I4.0 cluster.

Locally embedded knowledge, accompanied by a strong presence of industry and assisted by proper governance management, facilitates the implementation of I4.0. The peculiarities of I4.0 impact also on the functioning of the cluster, as they require a more inter-disciplinary and integrative approach, with the provision of ICs and development of related varieties. The natural processes of *stretching* the cluster cannot be prevented but should be harnessed for upgrading the core competences of the cluster. Due to digital transformation, clusters might evolve towards being providers of ICs and hubs of related varieties. The case of the HAv also appears to reflect this evolution.

Digital Transformation and Cluster Evolution

The analysis of the cluster's role in business digital transformation, and its reverse impact on the cluster based on the HAv case, yields exciting insight, as it highlights the need for a nuanced understanding of discussed categories (Figure 7.4):

1. First, the cluster contribution to the development of I4.0 processes could derive from the *CO* involvement/cluster initiatives (Sölvell, 2015; Ketels, 2004); with the co-ordinated actions being initiated by the managing authorities, rather than purely cluster features and assets. Even the ambiguous isomorphism, attributed to clusters and usually associated with inertia (Pinkse, Vernay & D'Ippolito, 2018), may be leveraged. Thanks to the collective identity and collective actions, the transition towards I4.0 can be legitimised and facilitated (Hervas-Oliver, 2019; Hervas-Oliver et al., 2019a).
2. Secondly, the impact I4.0 might exercise upon clusters should not be limited to technology, according to the narrow definition of I4.0.

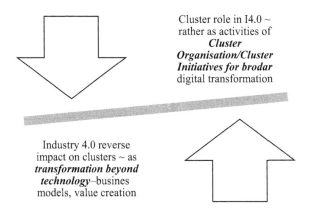

Figure 7.4 The (digital) transformation-induced future-oriented (cluster) transformation

Source: Author's own proposal

It can instead materialise, thanks to the broader implications, such as the changes of *value creation* (Nambisan, Lyytinen, Majchrzak & Song, 2017; Teece, 2017) *and business models*—still rather an under-researched area of I4.0 (Spaini et al., 2019). On the one hand, digital transformation can be understood in terms of a disruptive BMI. On the other, it requires itself to be the BMI, as the most difficult and challenging type of changes, as compared to product and service innovations (Ulrich & Fibitz, 2019; Amit & Zott, 2001). I4.0-related BMI encompasses, among others: service orientation, a partners' network and customer-oriented production or integration, personalisation and flexibility (Ibarra, Ganzarain & Igartua, 2018). It should also be stressed, that I4.0 presence has come in HAv in many forms, reflecting perhaps the 'interpretative flexibility' (Vernay, D'Ippolito & Pinkse, 2018): (1) various *bodies* work on it and implement it—ZAL in terms of technologies, HCAT+ in terms of educational needs, Airbus—as one of the major players, a user, and adopter of these solutions. (2) I4.0 as the *topic of* international co-operation encompasses such dimensions, such as R&R projects, HR co-operation, or collaboration in supply chain access. Finally, (3), I4.0 is regarded as both an *instrument* facilitating distant collaboration and the topic of such co-operation (knowledge).

Hence, the digital transformation stimulates the cluster transformation 'sensu largo'. It facilitates business sophistication and affects future-readiness, understood as the level of preparedness to exploit digital transformation, which encompasses adaptive attitudes, business agility and IT integration (The 2017 IMD World Digital Competitiveness Ranking). I4.0 also assists the cluster in the self-discovery, which is critical for competitiveness and structural transformation. Clusters contribute to this transformation, as the case of HAv shows, not only by its intrinsic features and attributes (knowledge base and business linkages), but also due to the CO's activities. The RV and ICs are provided and the processes of *stretching* take place, thanks to organised initiatives, such as supply chain excellence, with other aviation clusters in Germany, moderated actions by local institutions (ZAL HCAT+) or the creation of co-learning spaces.

The process taking place in HAv seems to have a resemblance to knowledge spill-overs, pertaining to the entrepreneurial ecosystems, where the shared knowledge base refers to the generic business process—i.e., how to organise effectively for entrepreneurial opportunity pursuit and BMI (Autio, Nambisan, Thomas & Wright, 2018). It mirrors the idea of GPT platforms, into which the clusters may develop (Cooke, 2017). Clusters in the I4.0 era might indeed morph and transform more into entrepreneurial ecosystems (Stam & Spigel, 2016). Whereas the previous clusters are chiefly defined as geographic concentrations of interconnected companies (Porter,2000); entrepreneurial ecosystems are conceptualised as a set of inter-dependent entities and various factors, which are co-ordinated in a way, enabling the emergence of productive entrepreneurship on the given territory (Stam, 2018; Stam & Spigel, 2016). It is possible for industrial clusters to be associated with established specialisation, but entrepreneurial ecosystems are linked with diversity and new specialisations. The cluster policy is about reinforcing existing industrial specialisations; while the entrepreneurial ecosystem policy aims at enabling industrial diversification. It would also be highly desirable to ascertain that the cluster poses the attributes critical for proper business ecosystems—sustainability, self-governance and capacity to evolve.

The studied concepts of *blending* and *hubbing* illuminate the need to see the evolution of clusters, as linked to the processes of scale and scope (Njøs et al., 2017 b).

I4.0 is a holistic topic, encompassing business models, mind-sets, value creation, not just technology. All partners along the value chain must adjust together in a standard way. As put by one of the HAv experts (CE2), 'Cluster can see more, has a better perspective, and it is even of more relevance as I4.0 is holistic—from design, innovation to recycling every element, and every partner should adopt'. The cluster seems to offer the right scale and be the right unit for change. However, they will have to re-define themselves, to continue providing value for their members.

I4.0 is about 'evolutionary revolution', and the cluster might be particularly well suited to advance it, as it offers the knowledge environment critical for major radical innovation (*revolution*), as well as a business eco-system, which is supposed to implement these solutions (*evolution*).

Advancement of I4.0 can be associated with disruptive technologies and revolutionary innovations. Implementation of the above often requires break-ing the existing lobby, which favours classic solutions. Thus, it requires joining forces, creating coalitions and speaking with one voice, and this is where the cluster can come in. It can offer unique value being an integrator of these solutions.

For many companies, the cluster can facilitate digital transformation by enabling efficient mutual learning from each other and allowing observa-tion. So, the cluster should have the 'content 4.0'. Too many members of the cluster are too small to do everything by themselves, so they need guidance and provision of information, to get partners.

In other words, it is not only the complexity of the holistic nature of I4.0 (along and across value chains), which makes the cluster pre-destined as a facilitating environment, but also the disruptive character of I4.0 (radical, breakthrough), which, for successful implementation, requires a joint col-laborative approach and coalition building.

As the cluster 'knows more', its task is to facilitate the challenge of I4.0, to be a vehicle for digital transformation, or as put by one HAv expert (CO1), 'to act as a key account manager to facilitate the I.40'. Nevertheless, 'clusters would change, due to digital business transformation, because the whole society would change; I4.0 impacts the cluster as it influences the lives of people'.

These megatrends cause a natural need for the cluster to adjust, to be able to fulfil its role. The impact of I4.0 on the cluster is tough to pre-dict. As put by one of the HAv members (CO1), 'clusters have been in the past and, I would think—they will continue, to be a useful tool, despite the digital transformation and obvious need to change business models'. The ability—diagnosed in the literature—to explore new knowledge, rather than only exploit it, would also become critical for cluster sustain (Gan-carczyk, 2015).

On the one hand, there are voices, claiming that the cluster, under the I4.0's pressure, would change, although, it would be an incremental pro-cess, step-by-step, done in an orderly fashion, visible in the content of meet-ings or their agendas. As put by one interviewee (CC6), 'the core of the cluster is networking, and that would be done today, tomorrow, the day after tomorrow'. On the other hand, as seen by some local experts, most likely this change will not be a linear process, but an exponential one, as I4.0 is all about radical change and disruptive technologies, implying far-reaching modifications. All in all, these ambiguous opinions seem to reflect the general confusing attitude towards I4.0—for some—the radical and revolutionary, for others—'only' evolutionary and gradual. Nevertheless, these two visions of cluster change can be reconciled. For even the far-reaching and non-linear cluster transformation would not happen overnight, but instead would emerge in a gradual process, co-shaped by the constituent cluster members (compare cluster role for incremental innovations—Hervas-Oliver et al., 2019b). How this transformation might violate the conservative nature of the cluster as a local and specialised phenomenon, remains to be seen. Likewise, the question if/how current regional clusters might evolve into entrepreneurial ecosystems is precisely thanks to the digital affordances (Autio, Nambisan, Thomas & Wright, 2018).

Digital transformation would re-shape clusters in the future. As argued by one company representative, (CC2) 'you still need personal contact, people around, meeting face-to-face, being introduced to each other, but affordances for the digital transformation offers, might make clusters morph into virtual states/digital villages'.

Clusters would need to re-invent themselves, think how they can 'destroy their business' (CC2). If they do not want to become redundant, they will have to. (CC2) 'Many benefits cluster provide now, can be replicated by digital transformation, so, clusters must shape the digital transformation, not be a victim of it'.

Distant communication and data exchange can indeed make co-location unimportant, and subsequently, pose an impending threat to the cluster. The cluster, therefore, needs somehow to bend under this pressure, by employing the tools the I4.0 offers. A cluster's importance and attractiveness, in times of I4.0, requires efforts, which in general, can be described as moving towards 'cluster 2.0', where classic properties are being enhanced by adding the modern digital tools. Thanks to modern digital tools, distant collaboration, exchange of data and sharing of knowledge are now possible, even from remote locations. Thus, it is the task of cluster managers to make them also work for the cluster; to harness them for agile internal CO. Clusters need to exceed and be superior to the rest, i.e. they need to out-perform, out-do and out-rival; they need to offer more than a general 'location-abstract or space-neutral' business environment can provide. Clusters need to be better than the rest—leverage the classic asset stemming from co-location and proximity, but add an extra layer, deriving from the opportunities brought about by I4.0.

As assessing the cluster development requires drawing on multiple dimensions and variables (number of firms, turnover, number of employees, patents granted, export markets, etc.), diagnosing the current stage in the cluster's evolution path is complicated. The more, as there is no consensus in the literature about how many, and which, precisely, phases of lifecycle should be distinguished (Valdaliso, Elola & Franco, 2016; Kury, da Rocha &

da Silva, 2019). In fact, there might be more possible trajectories of cluster development than one lifecycle.

As argued by Bergman (2008), a cluster can experience a renaissance with re-adjustment and re-structuring. A cluster can provide networking (via setting up neutral platforms), which is critical for advancing I4.0. Nevertheless, this digital transformation, alongside some other trends, can lead to the emergence of new areas of activity, such as UAM, leading to cluster modification and renewal. It was beyond the scope of this volume to analyse and establish the current stage of the HAv lifecycle. Nevertheless, the digital transformation might have already contributed to its renewal. As argued by one expert (CE4), 'in the past, we did not see many start-ups in the aerospace industry, and that has changed. It is partly because digitalisation makes it easier for smaller companies to participate, and they can contribute to a bigger network in a model, independent way'.

Only with some time lags can certain stages be diagnosed. How the digital transformation will play out on the HAv life cycle, and in general, how the I4.0 might affect the existence of many industrial clusters remains to be seen. It is too early to diagnose whether this I4.0 impact might provide a unique opportunity for the continuous 'ongoing change' (upward slope). It could result in the cluster renewal (Trippl & Tödtling, 2008) associated with incremental change (as some HAv members see it). It may lead to diversification (inclusion of new activities without abandoning the original one), or instead, to radical change (as some HAv experts predict with drastic modifications). 'Shifting sands in supply chains' encompass the development of UAM with air taxis, drones (UAV), electric propulsion systems or the likely return of supersonic planes (55th HAv Forum, 2019). It would also be interesting to see how these new trends would impact on cluster evolution. In particular, how the current hype about UAM would normalise at some point and how to make this new trend sustainable in the long run, by providing the right infrastructure, developing certificates and technologies, considering the aerospace industry's integrity and by accounting for social acceptance.

Part IV
Final Word

8 Conclusions

Cluster and I4.0 Relations Framed in ICs, RV and Stretching

By focusing on the case study, this volume addresses the calls for a more context-sensitive approach to cluster change and combines insight from technological change and the regional economy. Firstly, it developed a conceptual framework outlining the functioning of the I4.0 cluster, which explains the antecedents of cluster attractiveness for I4.0, and the consequences I4.0 would have on clusters. Based on the exploration of it's OWL cluster, it argues that locally embedded knowledge, accompanied by a strong presence of industry and assisted by proper governance management, facilitates the implementation of I4.0. The idiosyncrasies of I4.0 also impact upon the functioning of the cluster, as they require a more inter-disciplinary and integrative approach, with the provision of ICs and development of RV. The natural processes of *stretching* of the cluster should be harnessed for upgrading the core competences of the cluster. The second case study of the HAv, framed in the previously developed conceptual scheme, yielded more detailed findings as to the nature of IC and RV, and the *stretching* process of I4.0 clusters. It revealed the importance of the forward-looking provision of skills for the next generations, as well as the co-existence of 'diversification within specialisation' and local 'specialisation in diversification'. It showed that *blending* might provide critical complementarity, and confirm the long-term competitiveness (compare similar results by Rocchetta, Kogler & Ortega-Argilés, 2019; Janssen & Frenken, 2019); while multi-scalar *hubbing* must be sustainable.

This research proposes a more nuanced view on cluster internationalisation, in particular, by contrasting this dominant view with *hubbing*. It can enrich the discourse about cluster balance of specialisation and diversification, and subsequently, fit into the ongoing debate about the superiority of either 'MAR or Jacob's externalities' by offering some qualitative and empirically grounded approach. Last, but not least, it can contribute to the strand of literature devoted to 'cluster commons' or 'cluster effects', by shedding light on cluster attractiveness during digital transformation, in particular, by exploring the provision of (future-oriented) ICs. This study touches upon the co-evolution concept, as it addresses the possible cluster modification due to I4.0. Hence, it is aligned with recent research on clusters, which accounts for their evolution over time (Abatecola, Belussi, Breslin & Filatotchev, 2016; Ter Wal & Boschma, 2011).

The first case study of the I4.0 and it's OWL cluster demonstrated that the cluster role in the I4.0 era would lie not just in assuring the provision of new technologies and competences, but also in the dissemination and broader availability of them. So, it implies a certain re-focusing to the concept of ICs. The integrative nature of I4.0 would entail, on the other hand, the need for cross-sectoral collaboration. Thus, it stipulates the growing importance of locally available RV. Clusters would change under the pressure of digital transformation. They would need to remain open geographically (*hubbing*) and more diversified sectorally (*blending*), but these processes should be seen, in fact, as a necessary upgrading of local knowledge, preventing the cluster's lock-in and assuring long- term competitiveness.

Much has been said about the need to develop external cluster relations, but less is known about internal diversification, in terms of fields of activities. This volume addresses this issue by exploring the delivery of RV and *blending* processes.

As the HAv case has shown, the provision of IC and RV, along with the processes of *stretching*, is influenced by the moderating effects of industry (i.e. its propensity to I4.0), key actors (size and power) and the universal nature of I4.0 technologies. The studied concepts of *blending* and *hubbing* illuminate the need to see the evolution of clusters, as linked to processes of scale and scope. The mutually reinforcing I4.0 and cluster transformations epitomise the co-evolution processes (Figure 8.1).

The risks for local communities, deriving from the adoption of advanced production methods, seem to support the idea that clusters might become obsolete in I4.0 time (Dalum, Pedersen & Villumsen, 2005). However, the HAv case stresses the necessity of developing RV or a moderate specialisation, rather than rigid specialisation (Gancarczyk, 2015), and a need for *blending* and *hubbing*. It warns against relying on one single leader firm and one specialisation. This case advocates actions to avoid lock-in resulting from isomorphism. It demonstrates the importance of reaching out to external knowledge and assuring some diversity within the cluster. The HAv case further illustrates that more diversification and openness are needed. As argued by Buxbaum-Conradi (2018), SMEs in the local cluster must diversify into neighbouring industries and provide cross-sectoral

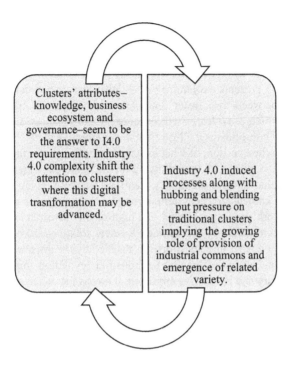

Figure 8.1 Cluster-I4.0-Cluster* relations

*-new updated cluster 2.0

Source: Author's own proposal

services and skills to reduce their over-dependency on Airbus. Undoubtedly, they should become more tied to networks and systems outside of the cluster.

This research juxtaposes the I4.0 attributes with cluster features, in order first, to clarify the role of the latter to the progress of the digital transformation, and second, to diagnose the likely implications of the fourth industrial revolution to the configuration of production systems, as currently characterised in clusters.

I4.0 cluster' might become an emblem to the old controversy, commonly referred to as 'MAR versus Jacobs'. It also could epitomise the incorporation of the concept of RV, introduced in an attempt to resolve an earlier empirical question, whether regions benefit most from being specialised or being diversified (Content & Frenken, 2016; Mudambi, Narula & Santangelo,

2018). RV assumes that inter-industry spill-overs occur mainly between sectors that draw on similar knowledge. Knowledge originating from one industry is most relevant to, and can most effectively be absorbed by, another industry that is related in the sense that firms draw on similar knowledge. Some 'diversity in unity' is, therefore, the recipe for economic growth.

This volume presents exploratory qualitative research investigating the relationship between the cluster and I4.0. It develops a comprehensive framework, which provides insight on clusters and business digital transformation and consolidates the results of the explorative study.

Concerning the question, of what exactly makes the cluster the right tool or place for advancing I4.0, and drawing on the gathered evidence, it may be confirmed that all three previously identified sources (i.e. the triple helix components), knowledge ecosystem, strong business presence and institutional framework, play a role. Stable and high-quality research in the region should be accompanied by the demand for new solutions from the active business and industry, and additionally, assisted by the governance structures. The peculiarities of the fourth industrial revolution imply a more inter-disciplinary and integrative approach. It means that what is needed are manufacturing and technical capabilities, facilitating innovativeness across industries, i.e. the ICs. Additionally, a cross-sectoral, holistic perspective and integration of different strands of engineering is desired, so that the benefits of RV can fully unfold.

Referring to the question of how I4.0 may, in return, influence clusters, and what kind of feedback on the cluster it may have, it may be presumed that I4.0, by its very nature, would stimulate certain behaviours and modifications, as it rewards an integrative and inter-disciplinary approach. The natural processes of expanding sectorally, and, to some extent also, geographically, i.e. the two processes of the so-called *cluster stretching*, may help to reinforce the fundamental core competencies of the cluster. They do not have necessarily to lead to some watering down of the existing hub of expertise, but rather should enable the upgrading of it. The issue of *stretching* seems the more important, as the digital revolution is being supposed to de-construct traditional industries and stimulate cross-industry convergence (*blending*) and allow further fragmentation and dispersion of activities (*hubbing*).

The case of HAv signifies the importance of *hubbing*. This geographical expansion can be regarded as a specific form of internationalisation, which aims to target and leverage foreign competencies or as a way of preventing the isomorphism. *Hubbing* and reaching out to explore and import external know-how and technologies, and thus, to bolster the key competencies, seem to be proactively sought after and initiated by CO, as a channel for safeguarding the ICs. *Blending*, which assumes some widening of the sectoral scope of cluster activities, contrary to what was initially expected, is not merely a reaction, a necessary adaptation to changes or a forced adjustment. It is promoted and supported with the aim to ensure the competitiveness, by enriching the existing RV.

Promoting provision of ICs and safeguarding the RV development, along with smart modelling of cluster *stretching* processes, might be seen as the new transformative place-based policy.

The Value Added of Presented Study

Industry 4.0 is supposed to transform the contemporary business models and development strategies, with far-reaching repercussions on societies, legal systems, labour markets and education. It has so far been studied, mainly from the company's or given sector's perspective, and in the context of the domestic economy. Presented research focuses on spatial aspects of the fourth industrial revolution. Thus, it enables the improvement of our understanding of complex processes and interdependencies of I4.0 and can provide new knowledge necessary for future scientific projects. Results of this research may add new insight to the discussed aspects of regional and development policies affected by the ongoing digital transformation and enrich the debate of whether such policy should be conceived as spatially blind, space-neutral or rather place-based.

Current thinking is that economic development does not happen, thanks to discrete projects, but emerges in interactive and dynamically adaptive ecosystems (Feldman & Storper, 2018). Thus, the critical issue becomes, how to create a local context, which facilitates the dynamic exchange of knowledge and experimentation, which does not penalise for failure and where institutions support the re-combination of products and processes. What matters is the local context for these processes, rather than the level of specialisation or diversification. The ultimate goal of provision of IC and RV should be regional development, adaptability and cluster renewal.

Drawing on the case study method, which focuses on the concrete cluster, and accounts for its idiosyncrasies, this volume can address the complaints about the too-standardised cluster and regional innovation policies. These policies result from popular benchmarking and learning from the 'best practice' approach. Thus, the provided case analysis fits into the advocated need of avoiding 'one-size-fits-all' solutions (Hassink & Fornahl, 2017).

Cluster policy, seen as part of regional development policy, stand-alone or aligned with smart specialisation, must not ignore the CLC. In contrast to static approaches, cluster policy should intend to sustain the long-term existence of the cluster, its resilience, adaptability and renewal. Understanding the peculiarities of the dynamics related to the emergence of subsequent growth, decline or transformation of clusters should encourage running policies, which are better adjusted to different phases of cluster development (Brenner & Schlump, 2011). It requires fine-tuning of current place-based, tailor-made, regional innovation policies. Fromhold-Eisebith (2017) proposes *clusterscape*, which comprises different cluster initiatives that focus on various economic sectors in the same region and provide favourable conditions for specific dynamics and advantages of collaborative learning. Inter-sectoral, intra-regional, collaborative learning, as present in HAv, epitomises such *clusterspace*.

Adaptability, renewal and the re-invention of clusters should be the motto for the future. Policy support must focus on changes of the cluster, integration of new knowledge, a fusion of sectors and technologies, emergence of new industries, the generation and use of variety. It needs to account for embeddedness in regional context, yet safeguard the openness and be geared towards expansion, while acknowledging the stages of development.

Findings of this study corroborate that clusters would need cross-innovation and internationalisation; to confirm their existence, they will have to mutate along RV (Cooke, 2017). They will transmute into different clusters or re-organise themselves as GPT platforms. Such technologies, also labelled as connecting, enabling or cumulative technologies, seem indeed to be central for I.40 (Qiu & Cantwell, 2018; Janssen & Frenken, 2019).

Against this background, i.e. the presence of the entire value chain and life cycle of aviation, as HAv boasts itself, an exciting research area in future study would be the analysis of the process of creating vertical spin-outs. Studies by Adams, Fontana and Malerba (2019) show that vertical spin-outs are an important part of the new entrants' population in related industries, and that they are more likely to survive than 'de novo' entrants. Vertical spin-out can be defined as an organisational structure, through which, knowledge is shared across industry boundaries. Thus, *blending* as a process enhancing the RV may happen not only via dedicated activities, such as bridging—co-learning and cross-clustering, but also by facilitating the spin-out emergence (Elekes, Boschma & Lengyel, 2019). The CFK valley in Stade—a spin-off/out cluster of Airbus group and HAv—provides an interesting example in this respect.

This volume tackles the issue of cluster dynamics, as it incorporates the ongoing fourth industrial revolution and accounts for I4.0 impact on cluster conceptualisation. Recent research clearly demonstrated that the static approach to clusters suffers many shortcomings, and a dynamic, evolutionary perspective is necessary (Belussi & Hervas-Oliver, 2016; Fornahl, Hassink & Menzel, 2015). There is a growing recognition among scholars about the need to symmetrically explore the death and decline of clusters (Bergman, 2008; Kury, da Rocha & da Silva, 2019; Martínez-Fernández, Capó-Vicedo &

Vallet-Bellmunt, 2012). In the opinion of Marafioti, Mollona, & Perretti, (2008)., it is the internationalisation, which could lead to de-population and the emptying of the cluster and result in 'declusterisation'. Bathelt and Taylor (2002) reckon that clusters contain the seeds of their own destruction and may potentially disappear or die. Lang (2009) argues that the erosion of cluster competitiveness, leading in effect to its decline, might originate in six negative forces. These are homogeneous macro-culture, problems with social identity, power imbalance, market rationalisation, a lack of untraded interdependencies and overwhelming negative externalities. In the light of the above, HAv efforts to reduce the asymmetry and power imbalance (related to the resource possession and central position in-network) should be particularly highlighted, as they also confirm the cluster's unique role to stabilise the relationships (Bathelt & Taylor, 2002).

This study explicitly takes up the issue of 'specialisation and diversification' of clusters. Existing research mainly states the nature of the cluster. It sees it as an agglomeration of value chain-related firms or local concentration of industrial firms and their support infrastructure, which are strictly inter-related through traded and/or untraded interdependencies (Fromhold-Eisebith & Eisebith, 2005; Bathelt & Taylor, 2002). However, it does not dwell more about the balance issue—i.e. the preferable proportions of diversification and focused specialisation. Exploring this perhaps normative question seems to be of even more relevance in the light of cluster evolution and lifecycle approach, which stipulates that a certain level of diversity (avoidance of too homogenous structures) is critical for cluster long-term existence and prosperity (Fornahl, Hassink & Menzel, 2015; Lang, 2009).

This volume also proposes a more nuanced approach to the process of the cluster's international and geographical expansion, by differentiating between internationalisation, in terms of foreign market expansion, conducted thanks to possessed competitive advantages in the form of FDI or export, while *hubbing* is seen as a geographic multi-scalar expansion, usually in search of sustaining or gaining a competitive advantage.

The study discussed in this volume adopted the relational research approach (Feldman & Storper, 2018), which integrates the context, path dependency and contingency factors. The obtained results are naturally, more authentic and empirically grounded and may serve as a departure point for prospective research. Findings limited to a specific industry must be treated with caution. Nevertheless, the conclusions might enrich our knowledge about the changing nature of industrial clusters, in the age of the fourth industrial revolution. This volume can enhance the scarce research landscape on geographical aspects of digital transformation, which is still eclectic and diverse (Castelo-Branco, Cruz-Jesus & Oliveira, 2019).

References

The 2017 IMD World Digital Competitiveness Ranking. www.imd.org/wcc/world-competitiveness-center-rankings/world-digital-competitiveness-rankings-2017/.

55th Hamburg Aviation Forum. (2019, June 5). *Ready for departure: Wohin Der Luftfahrtstandort Hamburg Fliegt.* Hamburg.

Aarstad, J., Kvitastein, O. A., & Jakobsen, S. E. (2016). Related and unrelated variety as regional drivers of enterprise productivity and innovation: A multilevel study. *Research Policy*, 45(4), 844–856.

Abatecola, G., Belussi, F., Breslin, D., & Filatotchev, I. (2016). Darwinism, organizational evolution and survival: Key challenges for future research. *Journal of Management & Governance*, 20, 1–17.

Adams, P., Fontana, R., & Malerba, F. (2019). Linking vertically related industries: Entry by employee spinouts across industry boundaries. *Industrial and Corporate Change*, 28(3), 529–550.

Alcácer, J., Cantwell, J., & Piscitello, L. (2016). Internationalization in the information age: A new era for places, firms, and international business networks?. *Journal of International Business Studies,* 47, 499-512

Aldrich, H., & Auster, E. R. (1986). Even dwarfs started small: Liabilities of age and size and their strategic implications. *Research in Organizational Behavior*, 8, 165–198.

Amit, R., & Zott, C. (2001). Value creation in e-business. *Strategic management journal*, 22(6-7), 493-520.

Anderson, J. C., Hakansson, H., & Johanson, J. (1994). Dyadic business relationships within a business network context. *Journal of Marketing*, 58, 1–15.

Asheim, B., Boschma, R., & Cooke, P. (2011). Constructing regional advantage: Platform policies based on related variety and differentiated knowledge bases. *Regional Studies*, 45(7), 893–904. http://dx.doi.org/10.1080/00343404.2010.543126.

Audretsch, D. B., Lehmann, E. E., & Menter, M. (2016). Public cluster policy and new venture creation. *Economia e Politica Industriale*, 43(4), 357–381.

Autio, E. (2017). *Digitalisation, ecosystems, entrepreneurship and policy.* Perspectives Into Topical Issues Is Society and Ways to Support Political Decision Making. Government's Analysis, Research and Assessment Activities Policy Brief, 20.

Autio, E., Nambisan, S., Thomas, L. D., & Wright, M. (2018). Digital affordances, spatial affordances, and the genesis of entrepreneurial ecosystems. *Strategic Entrepreneurship Journal*, 12(1), 72–95.

Autio, E., & Thomas, L. D. W. (2016). Ecosystem value co-creation. Imperial College Business School *Working papers: 28*. London. UK

Aznar-Sanchez, J. A., & Carretero-Gómez, A. (2016). Multinational corporations and cluster evolution: The case of Cosentino in the Spanish marble cluster. In F. Belussi & J. L. Hervas-Oliver (Eds.), *Unfolding cluster evolution*. Abingdon, UK: Routledge.

Baglieri, D., Cinici, M. C., & Mangematin, V. (2012). Rejuvenating clusters with 'sleeping anchors': The case of nanoclusters. *Technovation*, 32(3), 245–256. DOI: 10.1016/j.technovation.2011.09.003.

Bailey, D., & De Propris, L. (2014). Manufacturing reshoring and its limits: The UK automotive case. *Cambridge Journal of Regions, Economy and Society*, 7(3), 379–395.

Barry, F., Goerg, H., & Strobl, E. (2003). Foreign direct investment, agglomerations and demonstration effects: An empirical investigation. *Review of World Economics/ Weltwirtschafliches Archiv*, 139.

Barzotto, M., Corò, G., & Volpe, M. (2017). Sustaining industrial districts by leveraging on global and local value chains: Evidence from manufacturing multinational companies. In G. Gereffi, V. De Marchi, & E. Di Maria (Eds.), *Local clusters in global value chains: Linking actors and territories through manufacturing and innovation*. London: Routledge Publishing.

Barzotto, M., & Mariotti, I. (2018). Inward FDI and skilled labour force in Veneto industrial districts. In F. Belussi, & J.-L. Hervas-Oliver (Eds.), *Agglomeration and firm performance* (pp. 63–82). Advances in Spatial Science. Springer International Publishing AG. https://doi.org/10.1007/978-3-319-90575-4_5.

Basile, R., Benfratello, L., & Castellani, D. (2003). Attracting foreign direct investments in Europe: Are Italian regions doomed? *Papers of Institute for Studies and Economic Analysis*. Centro Studi Luca d'Agliano Development Studies Working Paper, 200. Turin, Italy

Bathelt, H., & Glückler, J. (2018). Relational research design in economic geography. In G. L. Clark, M. P. Feldman, M. S. Gertler, & D. Wójcik (Eds.), *The new Oxford handbook of economic geography*. Oxford University Press, UK

Bathelt, H., & Li, P.-F. (2014). Global cluster networks: Foreign direct investment flows from Canada to China. *Journal of Economic Geography*, 14, 45–71.

Bathelt, H., Malmberg, A., & Maskell, P. (2004). Clusters and knowledge: Local buzz, global pipelines and the process of knowledge creation. *Progress in Human Geography*, 28(1), 31–56.

Bathelt, H., & Taylor, M. (2002). Clusters, power and place: Inequality and local growth in time-space. *Geografiska Annaler: Series B, Human Geography*, 84(2), 93–109.

Baum, J. A., & Oliver, C. (1991). Institutional linkages and organizational mortality. *Administrative Science Quarterly*, 187–218.

Belderbos, R., & Carree, M. (2002). *The location of Japanese investments in China: Agglomeration effects, Keiretsu, and firm heterogeneity*. NIBOR Research Memorandum RM/00/02, University of Maastricht, Maastricht, the Netherlands.

Bellandi, M., Chaminade, C., & Plechero, M. (2018). *Transformation paths and the multi-scalarity of knowledge bases under Industry 4.0 challenges (No. 2018/14)*. Lund University, CIRCLE-Center for Innovation, Research and Competences in the Learning Economy, Lund, Sweden.

Belussi, F., & Hervas-Oliver, J. L. (Eds.). (2016). *Unfolding cluster evolution.* Abingdon, UK: Routledge.

Benitez, G., Ferreira Lima, M., Lerman, L., & Frank, A. (2019). Understanding Industry 4.0: Definitions and insights from a cognitive map analysis. *Brazilian Journal of Operations & Production Management*, 16(2), 192–200.

Benner, M. (2017). Smart specialization and cluster emergence: Elements of evolutionary regional policies. In *The life cycle of clusters: A policy perspective.* Edward Elgar Publishing, Cheltenham UK, Northampton MA USA.

Bergman, E. M. (2008). Cluster life-cycles: An emerging synthesis. *Handvolume of Research on Cluster Theory*, 1, 114–132.

Boschma, R. (2014). Constructing regional advantage and smart specialization: Comparisons of two European policy concepts. *Italian Journal of Regional Science (Scienze Regionali)*, 13(1), 51–68.

Boschma, R., & Giannelle, C. (2014). *Regional branching and smart specialisation policy.* JRC Technical Reports, S3 Policy Briefings No. 06/2014, European Commission, Seville, Spain.

Boschma, R., & Frenken, K. (2011). The emerging empirics of evolutionary economic geography. *Journal of Economic Geography*, 11(2), 295–307.

Boschma, R., & Iammarino, S. (2007). Related variety and regional growth in Italy. *Science and Technology Policy Research*, 62, 1–24.

Boschma, R., & Iammarino, S. (2009). Related variety, trade linkages, and regional growth in Italy. *Economic Geography*, 85(3), 289–311. http://dx.doi.org/10.1111/j.1944-8287.2009.01034.x.

Bourke, J., & Roper, S. (2019, June 19–21). Industry 4.0 is coming: The role of ambition in digital adoption by micro-businesses. Paper to be presented at *DRUID19 Copenhagen Business School.* Copenhagen, Denmark.

Bramanti, A. (2016). *New manufacturing trends in developed regions.* Three Delineations of New Industrial Policies: 'Phoenix Industry', 'Industry 4.0', and 'Smart Specialisation', Working Paper. www.certet.unibocconi.it. DOI: 10.13140/RG.2.2.30402.99522. www.researchgate.net/publication/307948547.

Brenner, T., & Schlump, C. (2011). Policy measures and their effects in the different phases of the cluster life cycle. *Regional Studies*, 45(10), 1363–1386.

Brettel, M., Friederichsen, N., Keller, M., & Rosenberg, M. (2014). How virtualization, decentralization and network building change the manufacturing landscape: An Industry 4.0 perspective, world academy of science, engineering and technology. *International Journal of Mechanical, Aerospace, Industrial, Mechatronic and Manufacturing Engineering*, 8(1), 37–44.

Brinkhoff, S., Suwala, L., & Kulke, E. (2016). Managing innovation in 'localities of learning' in Berlin and Seville. *Understanding Innovation in Emerging Economic Spaces*, 11–32.

Buciuni, G., & Pisano, G. P. (2015). *Can Marshall's clusters survive globalization?* Harward Business School Working Paper, 15-088. Boston, US.

Bureš, V. (2018). Industry 4.0 from the systems engineering perspective: Alternative holistic framework development. In *Analyzing the impacts of Industry 4.0 in modern business environments* (pp. 199–223). IGI Global. Pennsylvania, US.

Bustinza, O. F., Vendrell-Herrero, F., Santini, E., Bellandi, M., & De Propris, L. (2017). *MAKERS: Paper on servitization on manufacturing*. www.makers-rise.org/wp-content/uploads/2016/04/Deliverable-1.2-protected.pdf.

Buxbaum-Conradi, S. (2018). *Global and local knowledge dynamics in an industry during modular transition: A case study of the Airbus production network and the Aerospace Cluster in Hamburg, Northern Germany*. PhD Dissertation, Hamburg.

Cainelli, G., & Ganau, R. (2019). Related variety and firm heterogeneity. What really matters for short-run firm growth? *Entrepreneurship & Regional Development*, 1–17.

Cantner, U., Graf, H., & Töpfer, S. (2015). *Structural dynamics of innovation networks in German leading-edge clusters (No. 2015-026)*. Jena Economic Research Papers, Jena, Germany.

Cantwell, J. (1989). *Technological innovation and multinational corporations*. Oxford: Basil Blackwell.

Cao, L., Navare, J., & Jin, Z. (2018). Business model innovation: How the international retailers rebuild their core business logic in a new host country. *International Business Review*, 27(3), 543–562.

Castelo-Branco, I., Cruz-Jesus, F., & Oliveira, T. (2019). Assessing Industry 4.0 readiness in manufacturing: Evidence for the European Union. *Computers in Industry*, 107, 22–32.

CFK-Valley. https://cfk-valley.com/en/association/club/.

Chandrashekar, D., & Bala Subrahmanya, M. H. (2019). Exploring the factors of cluster linkages that influence innovation performance of firms in a cluster. *Economics of Innovation and New Technology*, 28(1), 1–22.

Chapman, K., MacKinnon, D., & Cumbers, A. (2004). Adjustment or renewal in regional clusters? A study of diversification amongst SMEs in the Aberdeen oil complex. *Transactions of the Institute of British Geographers*, 29, 382–396.

Charmaz, K. (2009). Shifting the Grounds: Constructivist Grounded Theory Methods for the Twenty-first Century. In J. Morse, P. Stern, J. Corbin, B.Bowers, K. Charmaz, & A. Clarke, *Developing Grounded Theory: The Second Generation*, Walnut Creek, CA: Left Coast Press. (pp. 127–154).

Cieślik, A. (2004). Determinants of spatial distribution of foreign firms in Poland. *Bank i Kredyt* (4), 55–70.

Ciffolilli, A., & Muscio, A. (2018). Industry 4.0: National and regional comparative advantages in key enabling technologies. *European Planning Studies*, 26(12), 2323–2343.

Clusters-Networks-International. www.bmbf.de/en/internationalisation-of-leading-edge-clusters-forward-looking-projects-and-comparable-1416.html.

Cohendet, P., Grandadam, D., Mehouachi, C., & Simon, L. (2018). The local, the global and the industry common: The case of the video game industry. *Journal of Economic Geography*, 18(5), 1045–1068.

Content, J., & Frenken, C. (2016). Related variety and economic development: A literature review. *European Planning Studies*, 24(12), 2097–2112. DOI: 10.1080/09654313.2016.1246517.

Cooke, P. (1992). Regional innovation systems: Competitive regulation in the new Europe. *Geoforum*, 23(3), 365–382.

Cooke, P. (2012). *Complex adaptive innovation systems: Relatedness and transversality in the evolving region*. Regions and Cities. London: Routledge.

Cooke, P. (2017). Eventually even attractive illusions come to an end: The death of 'Monitor' and demise of 'clusters'? In D. Fornahl & R. Hassink (Eds.), *The life cycle of clusters: A policy perspective*. Edward Elgar Publishing Cheltenham UK, Northampton MA USA.

Cooke, P. (2018). Generative growth with 'thin' globalization: Cambridge's crossover model of innovation. *European Planning Studies*, 26(9), 1815–1834.

Cooke, P., Uranga, M. G., & Etxebarria, G. (1997). Regional innovation systems: Institutional and organisational dimensions. *Research Policy*, 26(4–5), 475–491.

Corbin, J. M., & Strauss, A. (1990). Grounded theory research: Procedures, canons, and evaluative criteria. *Qualitative Sociology*, 13(1), 3–21.

Corbin, J. M., & Strauss, A. (2008). *Basics of qualitative research: Techniques and Procedures for Developing Grounded Theory* (3rd ed.). Thousand Oaks, CA: Sage.

Corrocher, N., & Cusmano, L. (2014). The 'KIBS engine' of regional innovation systems: Empirical evidence from European regions. *Regional Studies*, 48(7), 1212–1226.

Cusin, J., & Loubaresse, E. (2018). Inter-cluster relations in a coopetition context: The case of Inno'vin. *Journal of Small Business & Entrepreneurship*, 30(1), 27–52.

Cusumano, M. A., Kahl, S. J., & Suarez, F. F. (2015). Services, industry evolution, and the competitive strategies of product firms. *Strategic Management Journal*, 36(4), 559–575.

Dahl, M. S., & Pedersen, C. O. R. (2004). Knowledge flows through informal contacts in industrial clusters: Myth or reality? *Research Policy*, 33, 1673–1686.

Dahl, M. S., Pedersen, C. O. R., & Dalum, B. (2003). *Entry by spin-offs in a high-tech cluster*. DRUID Working Paper, 11, Copenhagen / Aalborg, Denmark.

Dalum, B., Pedersen, C. Ø., & Villumsen, G. (2005). Technological life-cycles: Lessons from a cluster facing disruption. *European Urban and Regional Studies*, 12(3), 229–246.

Delgado, M., Porter, M. E., & Stern, S. (2015). Defining clusters of related industries. *Journal of Economic Geography*, 16(1), 1–38.

De Marchi, V., & Di Maria, E. (2019). *Sustainability strategies, investments in industry 4.0 and cicular economy results (No. 0231)*. Marco Fanno Working Papers, 231. Dipartimento di Scienze Economiche, Padova, Italay

Desrochers, P., & Sautet, F. (2004). Cluster-based economic strategy, facilitation policy and the market process. *The Review of Austrian Economics*, 17(2–3), 233–245.

Deutschlands Spitzencluster Germany's leading-edge clusters. (2014). Bundesministerium für Bildung und Forschung (BMBF) Referat Neue Instrumente und Programme der Innovationsförderung, Berlin, Germany.

Die Luftfahrt-Branche in der Metropolregion Hamburg/The Aviation Sector In The Metropolitan Region Of Hamburg. (2019, Mai). Report by the VDI/VDE Institute for Innovation and Technology and Hamburg Aviation, courtesy of HAv; Hamburg, Germany.

Dierickx, I., & Cool, K. (1989). Asset stock accumulation and sustainability of competitive advantage. *Management Science*, 35(12), 1504–1511.

Dimache, A., & Roche, T. (2013). A decision methodology to support servitisation of manufacturing. *International Journal of Operations & Production Management*, 33(11/12), 1435–1457.

Dohse, D. (2007). Cluster-based technology policy: The German experience. *Industry and Innovation*, 14(1), 69–94.

Dohse, D., Fornahl, D., & Vehrke, J. (2018). Fostering place-based innovation and internationalization: The new turn in German technology policy. *European Planning Studies*, 26(6), 1137–1159.

Dominguez, N., & Mayrhofer, U. (2017). Internationalization stages of traditional SMEs: Increasing, decreasing and re-increasing commitment to foreign markets. *International Business Review*, 26(6), 1051–1063.

Drewello, H., Bouzar, M., & Helfer, M. (Eds.). (2016). *Clusters as a driving power of the European economy*. Baden-Baden: Nomos.

Duranton, G. (2011). California dreamin: The feeble case for cluster policies. *Review of Economic Analysis*, 3(1), 3–45.

EACP. www.eacp-aero.eu/about-eacp/mission.html.

Eisenhardt, K. M. (1989). Building theories from case study research. *Academy of Management Review*, 14(4), 532–550.

Eisenhardt, K. M. (1991). Better stories and better constructs: The case for rigor and comparative logic. *Academy of Management Review*, 16(3), 620–627.

Eisenhardt, K. M., & Graebner, M. E. (2007). Theory building from cases: Opportunities and challenges. *Academy of Management Journal*, 50(1), 25–32.

Elekes, Z., Boschma, R., & Lengyel, B. (2019). Foreign-owned firms as agents of structural change in regions. *Regional Studies*, 1–11.

Elola, A., Valdaliso, J. M., Franco, S., & López, S. M. (2017). Public policies and cluster life cycles: Insights from the Basque Country experience. *European Planning Studies*, 25(3), 539–556. DOI: 10.1080/09654313.2016.1248375.

Elola, A., Valdaliso, J. M., & López, S. (2013). The competitive position of the Basque aeroespatial cluster in global value chains: A historical analysis. *European Planning Studies*, 21(7), 1029–1045.

Engel, J. S. (2014). Clusters of innovation: Final thoughts. In J. S. Engel (Ed.), *Global clusters of innovation: Entrepreneurial engines of economic growth around the world* (pp. 378–390). Edward Elgar Publishing, Cheltenham UK, Northampton MA USA.

Etzkowitz, H. (2012). Triple helix clusters: Boundary permeability at university-industry-government interfaces as a regional innovation strategy. *Environment and Planning C: Government and Policy*, 30(5), 766–779.

Fallick, B., Fleischman, C. A., & Rebitzer, J. B. (2006). Job-hopping in Silicon Valley: Some evidence concerning the microfoundations of a high-technology cluster. *The Review of Economics and Statistics*, 88(3), 472–481.

Feldman, M., Siegel, D. S., & Wright, M. (2019). New developments in innovation and entrepreneurial ecosystems. *Industrial and Corporate Change*, 1–10. https://doi.org/10.1093/icc/dtz031.

Feldman, M., & Storper, M. (2018). Economic growth and economic development: Geographical dimensions, definition, and disparities. In *The new Oxford handbook of economic geography* (p. 143), Oxford University Press, UK.

Ferreira, J. J., Raposo, M., Rutten, R., & Varga, A. (2014). *Cooperation, clusters, and knowledge transfer: Universities and firms towards regional competitiveness*. Springer. Heidelberg, New York Dordrecht London

Fetzer, T., Schweitzer, H., & Peitz, M. (2017). *Bausteine für einen sektorenübergreifenden institutionellen Ordnungsrahmen für die Digitale Wirtschaft (No. 18-026)*. ZEW Discussion Papers, Mannheim, Germany.

Firgo, M., & Mayerhofer, P. (2018). (Un) related variety and employment growth at the sub-regional level. *Papers in Regional Science*, 97(3), 519–547.

Fitjar, R. D., & Timmermans, B. (2019). Relatedness and the resource curse: Is there a liability of relatedness? *Economic Geography*, 95(3), 231–255.

Fletcher, M., & Plakoyiannaki, E. (2011). Case selection in international business: Key issues and common misconceptions. In *Rethinking the case study in international business and management research* (p. 171). Edward Elgar Publishing. Cheltenham UK Northampton MA USA.

Fletcher, M., Zhao, Y., Plakoyiannaki, E., & Buck, T. (2018). Three pathways to case selection in international business: A twenty year review, analysis and synthesis. *International Business Review*, 27(4), 755–766.

Fløysand, A., Jakobsen, S.-E., & Bjarnar, O. (2012). The dynamism of clustering: Interweaving material and discursive processes. *Geoforum*, 43(5), 948–958.

Flyvbjerg, B. (2006). Five misunderstandings about case-study research. *Qualitative Inquiry*, 12(2), 219–245.

Foray, D. (2014). *Smart specialisation: Opportunities and challenges for regional innovation policy*. Abingdon, UK: Routledge.

Foray, D., David, P. A., & Hall, B. (2009). Smart specialisation: The concept. *Knowledge Economists Policy Brief*, 9(85), 100.

Fornahl, D., & Hassink, R. (Eds.). (2017). *The life cycle of clusters: A policy perspective*. Edward Elgar Publishing, Cheltenham UK Northampton MA USA.

Fornahl, D., Hassink, R., & Menzel, M. P. (2015). Broadening our knowledge on cluster evolution. *European Planning Studies*, 23(10), 1921–1931.

Franco, M., & Esteves, L. (2020). Inter-clustering as a network of knowledge and learning: Multiple case studies. *Journal of Innovation & Knowledge*. 5(1), 39-49.

Fratesi, U., & Rodríguez-Pose, A. (2016). The crisis and regional employment in Europe: What role for sheltered economies? *Cambridge Journal of Regions, Economy and Society*, 9(1), 33–57.

Fredin, S., Miörner, J., & Jogmark, M. (2019). Developing and sustaining new regional industrial paths: Investigating the role of 'outsiders' and factors shaping long-term trajectories. *Industry and Innovation*, 26(7), 795–819.

Freedman, M. L. (2008). Job hopping, earnings dynamics, and industrial agglomeration in the software publishing industry. *Journal of Urban Economics*, 64(3), 590–600.

Frenken, K., Van Oort, F., & Verburg, T. (2007). Related variety, unrelated variety and regional economic growth. *Regional Studies*, 41(5), 685–697.

Fromhold-Eisebith, M. (2017). Intra-regional collaborative learning between cluster initiatives: A factor of cluster (policy) dynamics? In *The life cycle of clusters: A policy perspective* (p. 95). Edward Elgar Publishing Cheltenham UK Northampton MA USA.

Fromhold-Eisebith, M., & Eisebith, G. (2005). How to institutionalize innovative clusters? Comparing explicit top-down and implicit bottom-up approaches. *Research Policy*, 34(8), 1250–1268.

Gancarczyk, M. (2015). Enterprise-and industry-level drivers of cluster evolution and their outcomes for clusters from developed and less-developed countries. *European Planning Studies*, 23(10), 1932–1952.

Gancarczyk, M., & Bohatkiewicz, J. (2018). Research streams in cluster upgrading: A literature review. *Journal of Entrepreneurship, Management and Innovation*, 14(4).

Gaschet, F., Becue, M., Bouaroudj, V., Flamand, M., Meunie, A., Pouyanne, G., & Talbot, D. (2017). Related variety and the dynamics of European photonic clusters. *European Planning Studies*, 25(8), 1292–1315.

Gausemeier, J., & Klocke, F. (2016). *Industrie 4.0: International Benchmark*. Paderborn: Options for the Future and Recommendations for Manufacturing Research.

Giannini, V., Iacobucci, D., & Perugini, F. (2019). Local variety and innovation performance in the EU textile and clothing industry. *Economics of Innovation and New Technology*. DOI: 10.1080/10438599.2019.1571668.

Gioia, D. A., Corley, K. G., & Hamilton, A. L. (2013). Seeking qualitative rigor in inductive research: Notes on the Gioia methodology. *Organizational Research Methods*, 16(1), 15–31.

Glaeser, E. L., Kallal, H. D., Scheinkman, J. A., & Shleifer, A. (1992). Growth in cities. *Journal of Political Economy*, 100(6), 1126–1152.

Glaser, B. G., & Strauss, A. L. (1967). Grounded theory: The discovery of grounded theory. *Sociology the Journal of the British Sociological Association*, 12(1), 27–49.

Glaser, B. G., & Strauss, A. L. (2011). *Status passage*. Transaction Publishers. New Jersey, US

Goerzen, A. (2018). Small firm boundary-spanning via bridging ties: Achieving international connectivity via cross-border inter-cluster alliances. *Journal of International Management*, 24(2), 153–164.

Götz, M. (2020). Primer on the cluster impact on internationalisation in the form of FDI in the time of Industry 4.0. *European Spatial Research and Policy*, 27(1), 195–220.

Götz, M., & Jankowska, B. (2017). Clusters and Industry 4.0: Do they fit together? *European Planning Studies*, 25(9), 1633–1653. DOI: 10.1080/09654313.2017.1327037.

Gouarderes, F. (2016). *Industry 4.0 European Parliament, PE 570.012*. Policy Department A: Economy and Scientific Policy. Commission Paper Green, Brussels, Belgium.

Grabher, G., & Ibert, O. (2018). Schumpeterian customers? How active users co-create innovations. In G. L. Clark, M. P. Feldman, M. S. Gertler, & D. Wójcik (Eds.), *The new Oxford handbook of economic geography, Oxford University Press, UK*.

Granovetter, M. (1985). Economic action and social structure: The problem of embeddedness. *American Journal of Sociology*, 91, 481–510.

Grillitsch, M., Asheim, B., & Trippl, M. (2018). Unrelated knowledge combinations: The unexplored potential for regional industrial path development. *Cambridge Journal of Regions, Economy and Society*, 11(2), 257–274.

Guimaraes, P., Figueiredo, O., & Woodward, D. (2000). Agglomeration and the location of foreign direct investment in Portugal. *Journal of Urban Economics*, 47(1), 115–135.

Hanse Aerospace. www.hanse-aerospace.net/en/association.html; www.hanse-aerospace.net/de/leistungen/digitale-projekte.

Hassink, R. (2016). Cluster decline and political lock-ins. In F. Belussi, & J. L. Hervas-Oliver (Eds.), *Unfolding cluster evolution*. Abingdon, UK: Routledge.

Hassink, R., & Fornahl, D. (2017). Introduction: Towards a more open and dynamic approach on cluster policy. In The Life Cycle of Clusters. Edward Elgar Publishing. Cheltenham UK Northampton MA USA.

Hassink, R., & Gong, H. (2017). Sketching the Contours of an Integrative Paradigm of Economic Geography, Papers in Innovation Studies Paper No. 2017/12. Centre for Innovation, Research and Competence in the Learning Economy (CIRCLE). Lund University, Lund, Sweden.

Hassink, R., & Gong, H. (2019). Six critical questions about smart specialization. *European Planning Studies*, 27(10), 2049-2065.

Hassink, R., Isaksen, A., & Trippl, M. (2019). Towards a comprehensive understanding of new regional industrial path development. *Regional Studies*, 53(11), 1636-1645.

HAv. www.hamburg-aviation.de/start.html.

HCAT. www.hcatplus.de/.

Head, K., Ries, J., & Swenson, D. (1999). Attracting foreign manufacturing: Investment promotion and agglomeration. *Regional Science and Urban Economics*, 29(2), 197–218.

HECAS. www.hecas-ev.de/.

Hermann, M., Pentek, T., & Otto, B. (2015). Design principles for Industrie 4.0 scenarios: A literature review, Working Paper No. 01, Technische Universität Dortmund www.snom.mb.tu-dortmund.de/cms/de/forschung/Arbeitsberichte/Design-Principles-for-Industrie-4_0-Scenarios.pdf.

Hervas-Oliver, J. L. (2019, June 19–21). The positive leverage of isomorphism: Endogenous collective action for transition into Industry 4.0 in industrial districts. Paper to be presented at *DRUID19 Copenhagen Business School*. Copenhagen, Denmark.

Hervas-Oliver, J. L., & Albors-Garrigos, J. (2014). Are technology gatekeepers renewing clusters? Understanding gatekeepers and their dynamics across cluster life cycles. *Entrepreneurship & Regional Development*, 26(5–6), 431–452.

Hervas-Oliver, J. L., Estelles-Miguel, S., Mallol-Gasch, G., & Boix-Palomero, J. (2019) a). A place-based policy for promoting Industry 4.0: The case of the Castellon ceramic tile district. *European Planning Studies* 27(9), 1–19.

Hervas-Oliver, J. L., Sempere-Ripoll, F., Estelles-Miguel, S., & Rojas-Alvarado, R. (2019) b). Radical vs incremental innovation in Marshallian industrial districts in the valencian region: What prevails? *European Planning Studies*, 1–16.

Hessels, J., & Parker, S. C. (2013). Constraints, internationalization and growth: A cross-country analysis of European SMEs. *Journal of World Business*, 48(1), 137–148.

Hidalgo, C. (2015). *Why information grows: The evolution of order, from atoms to economies.* New York: Basic Volumes.

Hintze, A. (2018). Entwicklung und Implementierung einer Cluster-Dachmarke-Konzeptualisierung auf strukturationstheoretischer Basis am Beispiel des Luft-fahrtclusters Metropolregion Hamburg.

Hüther, M. (2016). *Digitalisation: An engine for structural change-a challenge for economic policy* (No. 15/2016E). IW Policy Paper, Cologne Institute for Economic Research, Cologne, Germany.

Ibarra, D., Ganzarain, J., & Igartua, J. I. (2018). Business model innovation through Industry 4.0: A review. *Procedia Manufacturing, 22,* 4–10.

Industrie 4.0. Volkswirtschaftliches Potenzial für Deutschland. *Studie BITKOM.* www.bitkom.org/.

Islankina, E., & Thurner, T. W. (2018). Internationalization of cluster initiatives in Russia: Empirical evidence. *Entrepreneurship & Regional Development, 30*(7–8), 776–799.

Its OWL: Officially available materials on www.its-owl.com/home/and obtained during the field study, study visit and thanks to the courtesy of and discussion and interviews with Its OWL representatives.

James, L., & Halkier, H. (2016). Regional development platforms and related variety: Exploring the changing practices of food tourism in North Jutland, Denmark. *European Urban and Regional Studies, 23*(4), 831–847.

Jankowska, B., & Götz, M. (2018). Does innovation trigger the internationalisation of clusters?: The case of polish boiler-making cluster. In *Agglomeration and firm performance* (pp. 47–62). Cham: Springer.

Janssen, M. J., & Frenken, K. (2019). Cross-specialisation policy: Rationales and options for linking unrelated industries. *Cambridge Journal of Regions, Economy and Society, 12*(2), 195–212.

Järvi, K., Almpanopoulou, A., & Ritala, P. (2018). Organization of knowledge ecosystems: Prefigurative and partial forms. *Research Policy, 47*(8), 1523–1537.

Johanson, J., & Vahlne, J.-E. (2009). The Uppsala internationalization process model revisited: From liability of foreignness to liability of outsidership. *Journal of International Business Studies, 40,* 1411–1433.

Jungwirth, C., & Mueller, E. F. (2014). Comparing top-down and bottom-up cluster initiatives from a principal-agent perspective: What we can learn for designing governance regimes. *Schmalenbach Business Review, 66,* 357–381.

Kagermann, H., Wahlster., W., & Helbig, J. (2013). *Umsetzungsempfehlungen für das Zukunftsprojekt Industrie 4.0.* Frankfurt/Main: Acatech.

Kale, S., & Arditi, D. (1998). Business failures: Liability of newness, adolescence, smallness. *Journal of Construction Engineering and Management, 124*(6), 458–467.

Kamble, S. S., Gunasekaran, A., & Gawankar, S. A. (2018). Sustainable Industry 4.0 framework: A systematic literature review identifying the current trends and future perspectives. *Process Safety and Environmental Protection, 117,* 408–425.

Karafyllia, M., & Zucchella, A. (2017). Synergies and tensions between and within domestic and international market activities of firms. *International Business Review, 26*(5), 942–958.

Kasabov, E. (2015). Start—up difficulties in early—stage peripheral clusters: The case of IT in an emerging economy. *Entrepreneurship Theory and Practice*, 39(4), 727–761.

Keeble, D., Lawson, C., Smith, H. L., Moore, B., & Wilkinson, F. (1998). Collective learning processes and inter-firm networking in innovative high-technology regions. Cambridge: ESRC Centre for Business Research.

Keeble, D., & Wilkinson, F. (2000). *High-technology clusters, networking and collective learning in Europe*. Ashgate. Aldershot, U.K

Ketels, C. H. (2004). All together now: Clusters and FDI attraction. fdi magazine, Financial Time, UK

Kiel, D., Voigt, K. I., & Müller, J. M. (2018, April). How to implement Industry 4.0? An empirical analysis of lessons learned from best practices. Conference Paper to be presented at *International Association for Management of Technology IAMOT 2018 Conference Proceedings*. Birmingham, UK

Kogut, B., & Zander, U. (1992). Knowledge of the firm, combinative capabilities, and the replication of technology. In W. Chung & J. Alcacer (Eds., 2002), Knowledge seeking and location choice of foreign direct investment in the United States. *Management Science*, 48(12), 1534–1554.

Koschatzky, K., Kroll, H., Schnabl, E., & Stahlecker, T. (2017). Cluster policy adjustments in the context of smart specialisation? Impressions from Germany. *The Life Cycle of Clusters*, 173–200. Edward Elgar Publishing Cheltenham UK Northampton MA USA.

Kuah, A. T. (2002). Cluster theory and practice: Advantages for the small business locating in a vibrant cluster. *Journal of Research in Marketing and Entrepreneurship*, 4(3), 206–228.

Kury, B., da Rocha, A., & da Silva, J. F. (2019). Internationalization and the tale of the cabo frio beachwear cluster. In *Contemporary influences on international business in Latin America* (pp. 125–153). Cham: Palgrave Macmillan.

Kuusk, K., & Martynovich, M. (2018). *What kind of related variety for long-term regional growth?* (No. 1834). Utrecht University, Department of Human Geography and Spatial Planning, Group Economic Geography, Utrecht, The Netherlands.

Květoň, V., & Kadlec, V. (2018). Evolution of knowledge bases in European regions: Searching for spatial regularities and links with innovation performance. *European Planning Studies*. DOI: 10.1080/09654313.2018.1464128.

Lafuente, E., Vaillant, Y., & Serarols, C. (2010). Location decisions of knowledge-based entrepreneurs: Why some Catalan KISAs choose to be rural? *Technovation*, 30(11–12), 590–600.

Lafuente, E., Vaillant, Y., & Vendrell-Herrero, F. (2017). Territorial servitization: Exploring the virtuous circle connecting knowledge-intensive services and new manufacturing businesses. *International Journal of Production Economics*, 192, 19–28.

Lang, J. C. (2009). Cluster competitiveness: The six negative forces. *Journal of Business & Management*, 15(1).

Langlois, R. (2002). Modularity in technology and organization. *Journal of Economic Behavior and Organization*, 49(1), 19–37.

Lazerson, M. H., & Lorenzoni, G. (2008). Transforming industrial districts: How leading firms are escaping the manufacturing cage. In *The Oxford handbook of inter-organizational relations* (pp. 31–60), Oxford University Press UK.

Lazzeretti, L., Capone, F., Caloffi, A., & Sedita, S. R. (2019). Rethinking clusters: Towards a new research agenda for cluster research. *European Planning Studies*. DOI: 10.1080/09654313.2019.1650899.

Lechner, C., & Leyronas, C. (2012). The competitive advantage of cluster firms: The priority of regional network position over extra-regional networks: A study of a French high-tech cluster. *Entrepreneurship & Regional Development*, 24(5–6), 457–473.

Leydesdorff, L. (2012). The triple helix, quadruple helix, . . ., and an N-tuple of helices: Explanatory models for analyzing the knowledge-based economy? *Journal of the Knowledge Economy*, 3(1), 25–35.

Liao, Y., Deschamps, F., de Freitas, E., Loures, F., & Ramos, L. F. P. (2017). Past, present and future of Industry 4.0: A systematic literature review and research agenda proposal. *International Journal of Production Research*, 55(12), 410–426.

Lorenzen, M., & Mudambi, R. (2012). Clusters, connectivity and catch-up: Bollywood and Bangalore in the global economy. *Journal of Economic Geography*, 13(3), 501–534.

MacKinnon, D., Dawley, S., Pike, A., & Cumbers, A. (2019). Rethinking path creation: A geographical political economy approach. *Economic Geography*. DOI: 10.1080/00130095.2018.1498294.

MAKERS. www.makers-rise.org/about/.

Malerba, F. (2002). Sectoral systems of innovation and production. *Research Policy*, 31(2), 247–264.

Malmberg, A., & Maskell, P. (1999). Localised learning and industrial competitiveness. *Cambridge Journal of Economics*, 23, 167–185.

Malmberg, A., & Power, D. (2006). True clusters: A severe case of conceptual headache. In *Clusters and regional development* (pp. 68–86). Abingdon, UK: Routledge.

Manyika, J., Lund, S., Bughin, J., Woetzel, J., Stamenov, K., & Dhingra, D. (2016). *Digital globalization: The new era of global flows*. McKinseyGlobal Institute. San Francisco, USA.

Maresova, P., Soukal, I., Svobodova, L., Hedvicakova, M., Javanmardi, E., Selamat, A., & Krejcar, O. (2018). Consequences of Industry 4.0 in business and economics. *Economies*, 6(3), 46.

Martin, R., & Sunley, P. (2003). Deconstructing clusters: Chaotic concept or policy panacea? *Journal of Economic Geography*, 3(1), 5–35.

Martineau, C., & Pastoriza, D. (2016). International involvement of established SMEs: A systematic review of antecedents, outcomes and moderators. *International Business Review*, 25(2), 458–470.

Martínez-Fernández, M. T., Capó-Vicedo, J., & Vallet-Bellmunt, T. (2012). The present state of research into industrial clusters and districts: Content analysis of material published in 1997–2006. *European Planning Studies*, 20(2), 281–304.

Maskell, P., & Lorenzen, M. (2003). *The cluster as market organization, no 03–14*. DRUID Working Papers from DRUID, Copenhagen Business School, Department of Industrial Economics and Strategy/Aalborg University, Department of Business Studies, Copenhagen / Aalborg, Denmark.

McCann, P., & Ortega-Argilés, O. (2014). The role of the smart specialisation agenda in a reformed EU cohesion policy. *Scienze Regionali 13(1), 15-32*.

McHenry, J. E., & Welch, D. E. (2018). Entrepreneurs and internationalization: A study of Western immigrants in an emerging market. *International Business Review*, 27(1), 93–101.

Mellor, S., Hao, L., & Zhang, D. (2014). Additive manufacturing: A framework for implementation. *International Journal of Production Economics*, 149, 194–201.

Menzel, M. P., & Buxbaum-Conradi, S. (2018, July 24–28). Digitization of production and the transformation of regional relatedness. The Example of the Compound Material Cluster in Stade/Germany, 113 in Volume of Abstracts of 5th Global Conference On Economic Geography 2018 (GCEG 2018) Dynamics in an Unequal World. University of Cologne, Cologne, Germany.

Menzel, M. P., & Fornahl, D. (2010). Cluster life cycles: Dimensions and rationales of cluster evolution. *Industrial and Corporate Change*, 19(1), 205–238.

Marafioti, E., Mollona, E., & Perretti, F. (2008). International strategies and declusterization: a dynamic theory of Italian clusters. In Proceedings of the 50th conference of the Academy of International Business, Milan.

Montresor, S., & Antonietti, R. (2019, June 19–21). Regional diversification patterns and Key Enabling Technologies (KETs) in Italian regions. Paper to be presented at *DRUID19 Copenhagen Business School*. Copenhagen, Denmark.

Morgulis-Yakushev, S., & Sölvell, Ö. (2017). Enhancing dynamism in clusters. *Competitiveness Review*, 27(2), 98–112. http://dx.doi.org/10.1108/CR-02-2016-0015.

Morrison, A. (2008). Gatekeepers of knowledge within industrial districts: Who they are, how they interact. *Regional Studies*, 42(6), 817–835. DOI: 10.1080/00343400701654178.

Mudambi, R., Narula, R., & Santangelo, G. D. (2018). Location, collocation and innovation by multinational enterprises: A research agenda, *Industry and Innovation*, 25(3), 229-241

Mudambi, R., & Swift, T. (2012). Multinational enterprises and the geographic clustering of innovation. *Industry and Innovation*, 19, 1–21. DOI: 10.1080/13662716.2012.649058.

Muller, E., & Zenker, A. (2001). Business services as actors of knowledge transformation: The role of KIBS in regional and national innovation systems. *Research Policy*, 30(9), 1501–1516.

Muscio, A., & Ciffolilli, A. (2019). What drives the capacity to integrate Industry 4.0 technologies? Evidence from European R&D projects. *Economics of Innovation and New Technology*. DOI: 10.1080/10438599.2019.1597413.

Nambisan, S., Lyytinen, K., Majchrzak, A., & Song, M. (2017). Digital innovation management: Reinventing innovation management research in a digital world. *Management Information System Quarterly*, 41(1).

Njøs, R., & Jakobsen, S. E. (2016). Cluster policy and regional development: Scale, scope and renewal. *Regional Studies, Regional Science*, 3(1), 146–169. DOI: 10.1080/21681376.2015.1138094.

Njøs, R., Jakobsen, S. E., Wiig Aslesen, H., & Fløysand, A. (2017) (a). Encounters between cluster theory, policy and practice in Norway: Hubbing, blending and conceptual stretching. *European Urban and Regional Studies*, 24(3), 274–289.

Njøs, R., Orre, L., & Fløysand, A. (2017) (b). Cluster renewal and the heterogeneity of extra-regional linkages: A study of MNC practices in a subsea petroleum cluster. *Regional Studies, Regional Science*, 4(1), 125–138. DOI: 10.1080/21681376.2017.1325330.

OECD. (2017a, March 27). The future of global value chains: Business as usual or a new normal. Working document of Directorate for Science, Technology and Innovation, Paris. (unpublished).

OECD. (2017b). *The next production revolution: Implications for governments and business*. Paris: OECD Publishing. http://dx.doi.org/10.1787/9789264271036-en.

Osarenkhoe, A., & Fjellström, D. (2017). Clusters' vital role in promoting international competitive advantage: Towards an explanatory model of regional growth. *Investigaciones Regionales: Journal of Regional Research*, 39, 175–194.

Owens, M., Ramsey, E., & Loane, S. (2018). Resolving post-formation challenges in shared IJVs: The impact of shared IJV structure on inter-partner relationships. *International Business Review* 27(3), 584-593.

Park, S. C. (2018). The fourth industrial revolution and implications for innovative cluster policies. *AI & Society*, 1–13.

Patton, M. Q. (2015). *Qualitative research & evaluation methods: Integrating theory and practice* (4th ed.). Thousand Oaks, CA: Sage.

Pereira, G., Santos, A. de P., & Cleto, M. (2018). Industry 4.0: Glitter or gold? A systematic review. *Brazilian Journal of Operations & Production Management*, 15(2), 247–253. https://doi.org/10.14488/BJOPM.2018.v15.n2.a7.

Perry, M. (2007). Business environments and cluster attractiveness to managers. *Entrepreneurship and Regional Development*, 19(1), 1–24.

Philbeck, T., & Davis, N. (2019). The fourth industrial revolution. *Journal of International Affairs*, 72(1), 17–22.

Pinkse, J., Vernay, A. L., & D'Ippolito, B. (2018). An organisational perspective on the cluster paradox: Exploring how members of a cluster manage the tension between continuity and renewal. *Research Policy*, 47(3), 674–685.

Pisano, G. P., & Shih, W. C. (2009). Restoring American competitiveness. *Harvard Business Review*, 87(7–8).

Pisano, G. P., & Shih, W. C. (2012). Does America really need manufacturing. *Harvard Business Review*, 90(3).

Porter, M. (2000). Location, competition and economic development: Local clusters in a global economy. *Economic Development Quarterly*, 14(1), 15–34.

Prahalad, C. K., & Ramaswamy, V. (2004). Co-creation experiences: The next practice in value creation. *Journal of Interactive Marketing*, 18(3), 5–14.

Puig, F. (2019). New insights regarding clusters and industrial districts. *Competitiveness Review: An International Business Journal*. https://doi.org/10.1108/CR-03-2019-0033.

Putnam, L. L., & Nicotera, A. M. (2009). *Building theories of organization: The constitutive role of communication*. Abingdon, UK: Routledge.

Qiu, R., & Cantwell, J. (2018). General purpose technologies and local knowledge accumulation: A study on MNC subunits and local innovation centers. *International Business Review*, 27(4), 826–837.

Rammer, C., & Spielkamp, A. (2019). *The distinct features of hidden champions in Germany: A dynamic capabilities view*. ZEW-Centre for European Economic Research Discussion Paper, 19-012, Mannheim, Germany.

Redlich, T., Moritz, M., & Wulfsberg, J. P. (2019). *Co-creation*. Springer. Cham

Rehnberg, M., & Ponte, S. (2018). From smiling to smirking? 3D printing, upgrading and the restructuring of global value chains. *Global Networks*, 18(1), 57–80.

Reischauer, G. (2018). Industry 4.0 as policy-driven discourse to institutionalize innovation systems in manufacturing. *Technological Forecasting and Social Change*, 132, 26–33.

Rezk, R., Srai, J., & Williamson, P. (2016). International configuration revisited: Assessing the impact of product and knowledge attributes and changes in technology on the choices available to firms. *Journal of International Business Studies*, 47(5), 610–618.

Richardson, C., Yamin, M., & Sinkovics, R. R. (2012). Policy-driven clusters, inter-firm interactions and firm internationalisation: Some insights from Malaysia's multimedia super corridor. *International Business Review*, 21(5), 794–805.

Roblek, V., Meško, M., & Krapež, A. (2016, April–June). A complex view of Industry 4.0. SAGE Open, 1–11. DOI: 10.1177/2158244016653987. sgo.sagepub.com. http://m.sgo.sagepub.com/content/6/2/2158244016653987.full.pdf.

Rocchetta, S., Kogler, D. F., & Ortega-Argilés, R. (2019, June 19–21). Smart specialisation in EU regions: Revisiting the effect of relatedness on regional performance. Paper to be presented at *DRUID19 Copenhagen Business School*. Copenhagen, Denmark.

Rothgang, M., Cantner, U., Dehio, J., Engel, D., Fertig, M., Graf, H., . . . Töpfer, S. (2017). Cluster policy: Insights from the German leading-edge cluster competition. *Journal of Open Innovation: Technology, Market, and Complexity*, 3(3), 18.

Rüßmann, M., Lorenz, M., Gerbert, P., Waldner, M., Justus, J., Engel, P., & Harnisch, M. (2015, April 9). Industry 4.0: The future of productivity and growth in manufacturing industries. www.inovasyon.org/pdf/bcg.perspectives_Industry.4.0_2015.pdf.

Santos, C., Mehrsai, A., Barros, A. C., Araújo, M., & Ares, E. (2017). Towards Industry 4.0: An overview of European strategic roadmaps. *Procedia Manufacturing*, 13, 972–979.

Saxenian, A. (2000). The origins and dynamics of production networks in Silicon Valley. In R. Swedberg (Ed.), *Entrepreneurship: The social science view* (pp. 308–331). Oxford: Oxford University Press.

Schmidt, S., Müller, F. C., Ibert, O., & Brinks, V. (2018). Open Region: Creating and exploiting opportunities for innovation at the regional scale. *European Urban and Regional Studies*, 25(2), 187–205.

Schüßler, E., Decker, C., & Lerch, F. (2013). Networks of clusters: A governance perspective. *Industry and Innovation*, 20(4), 357–377.

Schuh, G., Potente, T., Wesch-Potente, C., Weber, A., & Prote, J. P. (2014). Collaboration mechanisms to increase productivity in the context of Industrie 4.0. *Robust Manufacturing Conference (RoMaC 2014), Procedia CIRP*, 19, 51–56.

Schurink, E., & Auriacombe, C. J. (2010). Theory development: Enhancing the quality of the case study as research strategy in qualitative research. *Journal of Public Administration*, 45(3), 435–455.

Schwab, K. (2017). *The fourth industrial revolution*. Currency. New York USA.

Sedita, S. R., de Noni, I., & Pilotti, L. (2015). How do related variety and differentiated knowledge bases influence the resilience of local production system? Paper in *Innovation Studies, No 20, CIRCLE*. Lund University, Lund.

Smit, J., Kreutzer, S., Moeller, C., & Carlberg, M. (2016, February). Industry 4.0: Directorate general for internal policies. Policy Department A: Economic and Scientific Policy. Ip/A/Itre/2015-02. Pe 570.007. Brussels, Belgium.

Smith, H. L., & Waters, R. (2005). Employment mobility in high-technology agglomerations: The cases of Oxfordshire and Cambridgeshire. *Area*, 37(2), 189–198.

Sölvell, Ö. (2015). Construction of the cluster commons. In *The Oxford handbook of local competitiveness* (pp. 84–101), Oxford University Press, Oxford, UK.

Sölvell, Ö., & Williams, M. (2013). *Building the cluster commons: An evaluation of 12 cluster organizations in Sweden 2005–2012*. Stockholm: Ivory Tower Publishers. www.regx.dk/fileadmin/user_upload/Orange_paper__3_.pdf.

Spaini, C., Rammer, C., Izsak, K., Sabanova, I., Romainville, J. F., Markianidou, P., Collado, A., Kroll, H., Wydra, S., & van de Velde, E. (2019). *Towards better monitoring of innovation strengths, regional specialisation and industrial modernisation in the EU*. European Commission, Brussels.

Speldekamp, D., Knoben, J., & Saka-Helmhout, A. (2019, June 19–21). A configurational analysis of firm-level innovation in European aerospace clusters. Paper to be presented at *DRUID19 Copenhagen Business School*. Copenhagen, Denmark.

Spieth, P., & Meissner Née Schuchert, S. (2018). Business model innovation alliances: How to open business models for cooperation. *International Journal of Innovation Management*, 22(4), 1850042.

Stam, E. (2018, February 22). *Entrepreneurial ecosystems & industrial diversification*. First European Cluster Policy Forum. Brussels.

Stam, F. C., & Spigel, B. (2016). *Entrepreneurial ecosystems*. Utrecht School of Economics Tjalling C. Koopmans Research Institute Discussion Paper Series, 16-13, Utrecht, The Netherlands.

Storper, M., & Scott, A. J. (1990). Work organisation and local labour markets in an era of flexible production. *International Labour Review.*, 129, 573.

Strange, R., & Zucchella, A. (2017). Industry 4.0, global value chains and international business. *Multinational Business Review*, 25(3), 174–184.

Suwala, L., & Micek, G. (2018). Beyond clusters? Field configuration and regional platforming: The Aviation Valley initiative in the Polish Podkarpackie region. *Cambridge Journal of Regions, Economy and Society*, 11(2), 353–372.

Szalavetz, A. (2019). Digitalisation, automation and upgrading in global value chains-factory economy actors versus lead companies. *Post-Communist Economies*, 1–25.

Teece, D. J. (2017). Towards a capability theory of (innovating) firms: Implications for management and policy. *Cambridge Journal of Economics*, 41(3), 693–720.

Ter Wal, A. L., & Boschma, R. (2011). Co-evolution of firms, industries and networks in space. *Regional Studies*, 45, 919–933.

Tinguely, X. (2013). *The new geography of innovation: Clusters, competitiveness and theory*. Springer. Hampshire UK.

Tödtling, F., Sinozic, T., & Auer, A. (2016). Driving factors of cluster evolution: A multi-scalar comparative perspective. In F. Belussi & J. L. Hervas-Oliver (Eds.), *Unfolding cluster evolution*. Abingdon, UK: Routledge.

Tödtling, F., & Trippl, M. (2005). One size fits all? Towards a differentiated regional innovation policy approach. *Research Policy*, 34(8), 1203–1219.

Trippl, M., & Tödtling, F. (2008). 12 cluster renewal in old industrial regions: Continuity or radical change? In *Handbook of research on cluster theory* (vol. 1, p. 203-218). Edward Elgar Publishing Cheltenham UK, Northampton MA USA.

Turkina, E., & Van Assche, A. (2018). Global connectedness and local innovation in industrial clusters. *Journal of International Business Studies*, 49(6), 706–728.

Turkina, E., Van Assche, A., & Kali, R. (2016). Structure and evolution of global cluster networks: Evidence from the aerospace industry. *Journal of Economic Geography*, 16(6), 1211–1234.

Tzeng, C. H. (2018). How foreign knowledge spillovers by returnee managers occur at domestic firms: An institutional theory perspective. *International Business Review*, 27(3), 625–641.

Ulrich, P., & Fibitz, A. (2019). Digitalisierung als Element der Geschäftsmodellinnovation. In Geschäftsmodelle in der digitalen Welt (pp. 233-248). Springer Gabler, Wiesbaden, Germany.

Uyarra, E. (2010). What is evolutionary about 'regional systems of innovation'? Implications for regional policy. *Journal of Evolutionary Economics*, 20(1), 115–137.

Valdaliso, J. M., Elola, A., & Franco, S. (2016). Do clusters follow the industry life cycle? Diversity of cluster evolution in old industrial regions. *Competitiveness Review*, 26(1), 66–86.

Valdaliso, J. M., Magro, E., Navarro, M., Jose Aranguren, M., & Wilson, J. R. (2014). Path dependence in policies supporting smart specialisation strategies: Insights from the Basque case. *European Journal of Innovation Management*, 17(4), 390–408.

Vanninen, H., Kuivalainen, O., & Ciravegna, L. (2017). Rapid multinationalization: Propositions for studying born micromultinationals. *International Business Review*, 26(2), 365–379.

Vargo, S. L., Maglio, P. P., & Akaka, M. A. (2008). On value and value co-creation: A service systems and service logic perspective. *European Management Journal*, 26(3), 145–152.

Vendrell-Herrero, F., & Wilson, J. R. (2017). Servitization for territorial competitiveness: Taxonomy and research agenda. *Competitiveness Review: An International Business Journal*, 27(1), 2–11.

Vernay, A. L., D'Ippolito, B., & Pinkse, J. (2018). Can the government create a vibrant cluster? Understanding the impact of cluster policy on the development of a cluster. *Entrepreneurship & Regional Development*, 30(7–8), 901–919.

Vicente, J. (2018). *Economics of clusters: A brief history of cluster theories and policy*. Springer.Cham, Switzerland

Visvizi, A., & Lytras, M. (Eds.). (2019). *Smart cities: Issues and challenges: Mapping political, social and economic risks and threats*. Elsevier. Amsterdam, the Netherlands

Welch, C., Piekkari, R., Plakoyiannaki, E., & Paavilainen-Mäntymäki, E. (2011). Theorising from case studies: Towards a pluralist future for international business research. *Journal of International Business Studies*, 42, 740–762.

Who makes SMEs ready for the digital future? (2019). Clustermanagement. www. its-owl.com/fileadmin/PDF/Informationsmaterialien/2019_Infobroschuere_EN_ inkl_Projekte_WEB.pdf.

Xu, S. X., & McNaughton, R. (2006). High-technology cluster evolution: A network analysis of Canada's technology triangle. *International Journal of Entrepreneurship and Innovation Management*, 6, 591–608.

Yin, R. K. (2009). *Case study research: Design and methods*. Los Angeles, CA: Sage.

Zaefarian, R., Eng, T. Y., & Tasavori, M. (2016). An exploratory study of international opportunity identification among family firms. *International Business Review*, 25(1), 333–345.

ZAL. www.zal.aero/en/news/.

Index

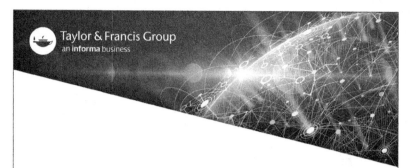

Printed in the United States
by Baker & Taylor Publisher Services